ERIC H.F. LAW

FEAR NOT

LIVING **GRACE** AND **TRUTH** IN A **FRIGHTENED** WORLD

**chalice
press**

Saint Louis, Missouri

An imprint of Christian Board of Publication

Other Books by Eric H.F. Law

The Wolf Shall Dwell with the Lamb:
A Spirituality for Leadership in a Multicultural Community

The Bush Was Blazing but Not Consumed

Inclusion:
Making Room for Grace

Sacred Acts, Holy Change:
Faithful Diversity and Practical Transformation

The Word at the Crossings:
Living the Good News in a Multicontextual Community

Holy Currencies:
6 Blessings for Sustainable Missional Ministries

Holy Currency Exchange:
101 Stories, Songs, Actions, and Visions of Missional and
Sustainable Ministries

With Dave Law
Drawing on Holy Currencies:
Awesome, Amazing, and Animated Activities for Stewardship

Available at ChalicePress.com

For my mother, Law Tam Un-Oi,
and my brothers and sisters:
Hung-Kwan Law, Maria Oi-Kam Ho, Stephen Hung-Fai Law,
Michelle Sau-Fong Ng, and Horatio Hung-Yan Law
for their unconditional love for me.

Cover design: Jennifer Pavlovitz

ChalicePress.com

Print 9780827211322
EPUB 9780827211339
EPDF 9780827211346

Printed in the United States of America

Contents

Acknowledgments

I am blessed by being part of a few trusting communities that enable me to be vulnerable, take risks, tell the truth, and experience intimacy. First of all, I thank my family, especially my mother and my brothers and sisters—Hung-Kwan, Maria, Stephen, Michelle, and Horatio—who exemplify unconditional love for me. They are the foundation I stand on each day of my life.

I am thankful for my "home" community at Sandpiper #3, Palm Desert, especially Dale and Nancy Hibler, Loraine Alvarez, Chuck McLucas, John and Pat Callender, Mary Kronman, Linda Clode, Michael O'Neill and Mark Hild, Bette and Jan Coffyn, Jim West and Karen Prinzmetal, Jon and Lois Jean Fults, Ruth Gray, Sue Brown, and Pat Griggs. From the moment I set foot in this community six years ago, I knew I would be safe and secure, with no fear of rejection or isolation. I am grateful for my colleagues and friends at the Kaleidoscope Institute for their commitment and passion for building open and accepting communities, especially Lilline Dugan, Peter Bechtel, Lynn Oshita, Lucky Altman Lynch, Alexandra Conrad, Dorothy Wilson, Keith Yamamoto, and Bonnie Rice. They have been there to help me face my fear during the transitional time of the Institute. I thank the bishops and staff of the Episcopal Diocese of Los Angeles and the Cathedral Center for their prayers and support for me and the ministry of the Kaleidoscope Institute. Their ministry creates a safe and gracious space for people to gather to explore the possibility of faithful transformation. I thank Kaye Ballard and Myvanwy Jenn for their constant friendship and support, Linda and Paul Kelly for love and support for Steve while I was working on this book, Kent Steinbrenner for his enthusiasm and knowledge of the English language, and my editor Trent Butler for his patience and understanding. I thank Steve Rutberg for being the intimate soul mate I come home to. Finally, I thank God for being my true security.

> In God, whose word I praise,
> in the LORD, whose word I praise,
> in God I trust; I am not afraid.
> What can a mere mortal do to me?
> (Ps. 56:10–11)

Preface

It has been more than ten years since the publication of the first edition of this book, then titled *Finding Intimacy in a World of Fear*. To be honest, I was disappointed at how little impact this book had made over the last ten years. I wrote the book as a response to the fear-based reactions to the September 11, 2001, terrorist attacks, and the way fear was used in subsequent years to motivate people to act in constructive and destructive ways—mostly destructive. My goal was to help readers to address fear in constructive and faithful ways. My hope was that these constructive analyses and processes would spread, at least through churches within the major denominations, to help reverse the ever-increasing fear trend in the United States. But the fear-exploiters and marketers continued to skillfully deploy their weapons, gaining power and money. Ten years after the initial publication of this book, I found myself living in a world where fear reigns supreme, regardless of one's political or ideological perspective: fear of politicians and government officials such as Trump, Obama, or Clinton; fear of government agencies such as the FBI, Department of Justice, and the White House Administration; fear of terrorism, disaster, climate change, immigrants, police, or people of color. The list goes on.

Meanwhile, intimacy—a time and place where we can be face to face with one another to share truth—especially among those who are different politically, racially, and economically, is getting harder and harder to achieve.

I was interviewing Scott Bader-Saye for another writing project. Scott published *Following Jesus in a Culture of Fear* around the same time that *Finding Intimacy in a World of Fear* came out. We were commiserating because we felt that our books were not having the impact that we had hoped. What we had both offered in our books was a rational, intellectual approach to fear. Yet fear is a powerful emotional and intuitive thing, and has been used from the beginning of human community to effectively motivate people for good and for bad.

Scott shared with me that he had been reading in the field of moral psychology[1] for his own research. He said, "Over the last five to ten years, these psychologists have consistently been telling us that most of our moral judgments are arising not out of reflection but intuition. People rarely make ethical decisions based on reason. It's a reaction out of intuition, out of their gut."

One of the authors Scott had read, American social psychologist Jonathan Haidt, said that while reason plays a role in moral judgment, it "is far less powerful than intuition, so if you're arguing (or deliberating) with a partner who lives on the other side of the political spectrum from you, and you approach issues such as abortion, gay marriage, or income inequality with powerfully different intuitive reactions, you are unlikely to effect any persuasion no matter how good your arguments and no matter how much time you give your opponent to reflect upon your logic.[2]

Scott also pointed me to the work of Bryan Stevenson, author of *Just Mercy*, who talks about the importance of proximity with his work among prisoners on death row. Stevenson proposes the following "four steps to really change the world":[3]

1. **We have to get approximate to the problems we care about.** Stevenson's point is that we cannot solve a problem at a distance. We need to get up close, because that "proximity" will help us to truly understand others—their experiences, perspectives, and possible solutions they may offer.

2. **We have to change the narrative.** Stevenson believes that U.S. culture is based on "a narrative of fear and anger." This rings true to me because so much of my work in facilitating gracious and courageous conversation begins with changing the narrative from a fear-based, debate model to a mutually respectful, community-building, story-telling scenario.

3. **We have to remain hopeful.** We may not be successful all the time, but hope keeps us going. Stevenson identifies hope,

---

[1]Scott named the following authors and books as his sources: Jonathan Haidt's *The Righteous Mind*, Joshua Greene's *Moral Tribes* and Daniel Kahneman's *Thinking, Fast and Slow*.

[2]Jonathan Haidt, "Reasons Matter (When Intuitions Don't Object)," *The New York Times*, October 7, 2012, https://opinionator.blogs.nytimes.com/2012/10/07/reasons-matter-when-intuitions-dont-object/ .

[3]Martin Saunders, "Bryan Stevenson: Four steps to really change the world," *ChristianToday*, July 16, 2015, https://www.christiantoday.com/article/bryan-stevenson-four-steps-to-really-change-the-world/59211.htm .

driven and enabled by faith, as the key ingredient in fighting injustice for the long term.

4. **Sometimes we have to do uncomfortable things.**

Scott said at the end of our conversation, "We tend to talk about others instead of talking to them in person. Left-leaning Christians need to connect with right-leaning Christians and say, 'Let me hear your story' and vice-versa. How do we come into proximity with each other without the posture of judgment or superiority? How do we express authentic curiosity toward those who whose opinions and views differ from our own, and not act as if we are there to study them as strange creatures who voted for the other person?"[4]

Achieving intimacy in a world of fear is not about using words and trying to reason our way in. Intellectual discourses are not going to get us very far without the context of face-to-face relationships and close proximity to each other. This will be uncomfortable because being in proximity with differing others will trigger our fears—fear of rejection, as well as fear of emotional and even physical harm. For this reason, changing the narrative away from fear and debate is essential; start with an invitation to enter into a gracious and brave space for dialogue and then introduce and affirm a set of respectful communication guidelines before any interpersonal engagement. In my book *Inclusion: Making Room for Grace*, I illustrate how to create a "grace margin." Creating a grace margin is my way of changing the fear narrative and preparing the way for an up-close encounter.

In this new edition, I have added suggested activities and questions for discussion at the end of each chapter. I invite my readers to create a grace margin and form small groups to read this book together. Invite the group to meet periodically, face-to-face, to do the suggested activities and share reflection on the discussion questions. Diversity within the group will make for more fruitful conversations.

I have also added a new chapter. My original thought for this chapter was to add my reflections on fear and intimacy gleaned from the last ten years. Instead I decided that I would let my readers do much of that reflection themselves through the discussion questions. So the additional chapter offers processes

[4]The full interview with Scott Bader-Saye is in *Companion on the Episcopal Way*, coauthored by Eric. H.F. Law and Stephanie Spellers, published by Morehouse Publishing.

and practical resources for individual exploration, and for bringing diverse people together in close proximity to do the uncomfortable thing—build relationship and share their truth. I also included lyrics of songs I wrote in the past year. You can find recordings of these songs on the Internet.[5] I have also included a dialogue process, "Prep for the Holidays," from Building Bridges Now—an Internet dialogue resource—in the Appendix to show you how to create a grace margin for courageous conversations at holiday gatherings, especially when politics come up. A second dialogue process, "Disaster Preparedness," is available to download from ChalicePress.com/FearNot. This session brings people together to address the fear, and plan responses to, a natural disaster. Hopefully these additional resources will help more people to live grace and truth in a frightened world.

> I am longing for a day of seeing without tears
> I am yearning for a day of living without fears
> A day when ev'ryone's free
> And no one's bullied to conform
> A day with no threats of war
> No shields, no armored uniforms
> A day with no flood or draught
> And no more man-made angry storms
> A day when truthfulness reigns
> And grace and kindness is the norm
> Come and dream with me
> For that day of seeing without tears
> Come and work with me
> For the way of living without fears.
> Come and walk with me
> Walk the way of justice and of peace
> Come and pray with me
> Pray for grace and courage without cease

Eric H. F. Law
May 2019

---

[5]You can find simple video recordings of these songs in my YouTube channel: https://www.youtube.com/channel/UCDtDLY83mHTSSsjkprJaF1g/ videos, and the songs are in an album titled *Up-Side-Down Town* by Eric H. F. Law available in iTunes, Amazon, CDBaby and other major music providers.

Introduction

I feel incompetent every year when April approaches, because the fifteenth of that month is the deadline for filing my income tax return. As a citizen of the United States of America, I have to report how much I earned in the previous year and pay taxes that support the U.S. federal, state, and sometimes city governments. You would think that someone like me, who got all As in my mathematics classes through high school and college, would be able to figure out how to fill out the income tax forms. Twenty years ago, I attempted to do my own tax return and gave up. I hired a tax preparer to file my income tax, and I have been using him ever since.

Each year, I collect all the receipts, bills, and pay stubs, add up the numbers, and put them into the simplified form that my tax preparer sends me. Then I send the form back to my tax preparer with all the necessary supporting documents. Miraculously, in a few weeks, an inch-thick package arrives in the mail. All I have to do is to write my signature on all the right places and put the proper forms in the proper envelopes. Gleefully, I paste stamps on the envelopes and put them in the mail. Usually, I do not even care about whether I get a refund or not. I am just happy to get it done, so that I avoid getting into trouble with my government. I then put the receipts, bills, pay stubs, and the copy of the income tax return forms in a box, label it, and put it away in a safe place so I can find it again, in case I get audited.

Just what am I afraid of? I am paying for my government to protect me and my community. Isn't that what paying taxes is about? But each year, the forms seem to get more and more complicated. For the year 2005, I had to file tax forms in eight states. To compound things further, I heard on the radio that if you input the exact same numbers in different computer tax-preparation programs, you can end up with different results. Well, how do I know I have gotten it right? Is my tax-preparer using the right program?

I think these complicated forms are there to make me feel incompetent each year and that they are meant to evoke fear. File

1

on time, make sure your numbers do not look suspicious, and hope to God that you will not get audited. Instead of feeling good about having paid the taxes, thereby supporting my government to keep us safe and secure, I paid my tax and was still afraid—not just about not being protected, but fearful of my own government, which would punish me if I did not do my taxes correctly.

The Cause of My Fear

Why was I full of fear? It was only money! If they discovered that I did not pay enough, I would just pay up and pay the fine too. If I could not pay back right away, I could create a payment plan to eventually pay it off. No big deal. Filing my tax late or incorrectly does not link me or my family to imminent danger. With the comfort of knowing that I was not in immediate danger, I reflected further on this fear.

Filing my income tax return is an annual reminder that I cannot trust myself and my ability to complete the necessary forms. Even if I employ a tax preparer or the latest computer technology to help me, I am reminded that they can also make mistakes. It also reminds me that my government does not trust me to do the right thing, so the Internal Revenue Service will randomly pick people to be audited. It also reminds me that I cannot trust my government to use my tax dollars properly. People of my generation are talking pessimistically about the future of Social Security. Don't count on getting your share when you retire. Therefore, I, and everyone I know, want to pay as little tax as possible without breaking the tax code. Filing my income tax form each year reminds me of the abusive cycle of distrust and fear between me and my government. Paying taxes becomes a rule and ritual that I must follow or I will be punished. I do it out of fear instead of love for this country and my trust for our civic leaders. I lose sight of the meaning of paying taxes. I lose connection with my government.

A Climate of Fear

The fear I feel around filing my income tax return is only part of the climate of fear that we live in today. It is obvious that since September 11, 2001, a fear of terrorist attacks dominates our minds. However, if we observe the messages that we receive every day through the media, marketers, and politicians, we would see that fear is projected constantly in the form of distrust of ourselves, our community, our government, and even nature.

One night of watching television will show us that we cannot trust friends and family. They can betray us, tell our secrets, and steal our loved ones. We see parents who kill their children and children who murder their parents. Fathers molest their children. We cannot trust our teachers or pastors; they can be molesters of our children too. We cannot trust our neighbors; they can be mass murderers. A terrorist cell can be right around the corner from where we live. We cannot walk down the street without fearing that someone is going to hurt us, rob us—or worse, murder us.

We cannot trust the institutions that were created to help us feel safe. Our police force is supposed to protect us, but how many scandals have we heard that involve the corruption of our police departments? Our courts of law are supposed to help us feel secure, because people know that they will be punished if they commit a crime. But we are also shown, time and time again, in crime-glorifying movies and television shows that if a criminal is smart or rich enough, he or she can get away with murder. We become cynical about our legal system because we do not really believe that it can keep us safe.

We cannot trust our government because the leaders (even though they are elected by the people to represent the people) are all politically driven—which means, to many people, that they are crooks and liars. They will say and do anything to get our votes. Once they get elected, they do whatever they want for their own gain. Not only are they not working to protect us, they often play on our fears to get us to vote for them:

- "If you do not want to feel the fear that you experienced on September 11, 2001, you should vote for me because I will keep the country safe."
- "People are addicted to nonrenewable fuel, which pollutes the air that we breathe and causes irreversible global warming that makes this planet uninhabitable. Vote for me and I'll do something about that for you."
- "If you let same-sex couples get married, that will destroy the institution of marriage. God will punish us for letting this happen. Vote for me; I'll do something about that for you."

We get opposing and conflicting information, all aimed at triggering our fear so that we will do what the different parties want us to do. Some of us are so confused that we end up not trusting anyone in our government.

We can't trust technology to keep us safe anymore. We have computers and the Internet to provide us with access to information, only to find out that this freedom of information can overwhelm us while providing our children with images and information that are harmful. Worse, Internet predators lurk out there, just waiting to get our children when they are most vulnerable. We have the wonderful technology of mobile phones, only to find that their invisible waves might give us brain cancer. We have created nuclear arms to keep us safe from our "enemies," only to find out that if someone makes one wrong decision, or if these weapons get in the "wrong hands," then these weapons can destroy the whole world. Whether these things are true or not, they send the message that we cannot trust technologies, which have been our best ally in addressing our fear.

We cannot trust nature, either. In the 2005–2006 period, nature provided us with hurricanes, earthquakes, tsunamis, tornadoes, floods, droughts, and unbearable killing heat. While I was writing this book, my editor in Tennessee lost his entire house to a tornado. We are told that some horrible natural disasters are being caused by our use of technologies, such as the emissions from our factories and automobiles. Some of us used to think that if we stopped messing with nature, nature would take care of itself, and of us. Now we are told that nature cannot recover quickly, even if we stop abusing the environment.

Life as Risk Management

In this world of fear, everything and everyone is at risk. Life is not about living anymore, but about risk management. For example, in this climate of fear, church is no longer about doing ministry and serving people. It is about minimizing the risk of the pastor or church workers being sued for abuse. It is about reducing the risk of being audited by the IRS for misusing their funds as a nonprofit organization.

Risk management is a reactive process based on fear. It is about distancing ourselves from others whom we have considered to be dangerous and suspicious. Managing risk is about what not to do in fear of being hurt or used. Risk management destroys intimacy because it is based on distrust. When there is no trust, there is no vulnerability. When there is no vulnerability, there is no truth telling. When there is no truth telling, there is no intimacy. When there is no intimacy, there is no community, which is human beings' primary support for facing their fears.

My Journey through Fear's Landscape

In this world of fear, we need to find ways to move from risk management to living in faith through Jesus Christ. Living in faith has to do with actively engaging people, the community, and creation in spite of our fear. Living the gospel is about trusting God, and trusting each other as children of God, so that we can be vulnerable, take risks, and tell the truth. And the truth will set us free to connect and be intimate with each other and with God. We need this kind of intimacy the most in order to develop communities of trust in which we can face the world of fear together.

This book is my journey through this landscape of fear. I try to understand the purpose of fear as an intuitive response to potential danger, show how fear can help us protect ourselves, and demonstrate how fear can lead us to discover our passion for ministry (chapter 1). Having affirmed the place of fear in our lives, I then explore how the media, marketers, and politicians use fear to get us to pay attention to them. In the process, we can be overwhelmed by the constant projections of fear all around us (chapter 2). Following that, I have looked into how we address our fear through rituals, rules, and technologies—and how, again, marketers and politicians can use these approaches to sell us symbolic substitutes that claim to make us safe (chapter 3). I then investigate the different roles we have been cast in within this arena of fear—the fear-conquerors, the fear-bearers, and the fear-exploiters. I show how God, through Jesus Christ, invites us to be fear-miners, mining gifts from our fear (chapters 4 and 5). I propose that intimacy developed in building trusting communities is the best way to prepare ourselves to address fear constructively (chapter 6). I illustrate this from the biblical story of Elijah and from my own personal experiences, showing that when I give in to fear, God comes and asks, "What are you doing here?, bringing me back to the divine mission and away from focusing on my own condition (chapter 7).

Through this journey, I was most excited when I was able to name the "powers" that have tried to separate us, destroying intimacy, and therefore evoke fear effectively to control others. My attempt to name these "powers" will hopefully help my readers to get a handle on what to do in order to not be controlled by fear-exploiters in our lives, communities, institutions, and nations, but to find ways to achieve intimacy in spite of the fear projected all around us.

Questions and Activities

1. Name some of the elements of the "Climate of Fear" described in the Introduction.
2. In what ways have you experienced the "Climate of Fear" during the past week? The past year?
3. What fears were triggered for you? What does the triggering of these fears lead you to do?
4. What is the difference between risk management and doing ministry?

1

Fear, Phobia, Sex, and Ministry

I went to an open house of a condominium for sale on the thirtieth floor of a beautiful building in Vancouver, British Columbia. It had a fairly good-sized balcony that, according to the realtor, was a major selling point of this property. Gingerly, I stepped onto the balcony, making sure that it was solidly built and that the floor was not wet or slippery. As I moved toward the railing, I noticed my heart was pounding a little faster. I pushed against the rail with my hand making sure that it was also secured before I would lean on it. I held onto the rail with one hand while my other hand automatically moved up toward my face. With my index finger pressing against my glasses to make sure they would not fall off my face, I looked over the railing and down. Cars, like toys, moved through the streets below. I thought to myself: no one would survive a fall from this high up. I looked out and saw the magnificent view of the city, with the snow-capped mountains serving as a backdrop. That view was why I stepped out on this balcony on the thirtieth floor.

The Nature of Fear

I have a fear of heights. I used to be embarrassed to admit it until I started doing research for this book. As I read many books on the subject of fear, I discovered that my fear of heights is normal and justified. Miriam Greenspan, in her book *Healing Through the Dark Emotions,* writes:

> Fear arises in any situation where there is a threat of loss or harm to body, mind, and spirit. It is a basic emotion, built into the biological organism. Part of our deepest instinct

7

for survival, fear is our emotion alarm system...Without
it, we would be unable to protect ourselves...What fear
tells us is that something requires immediate and close
attention. Its purpose is to move us to action to protect
life. An alarm signal goes off that says: Stop where you
are—there's danger ahead.[1]

Gavin de Becker, author of *The Gift of Fear,* describes fear as an
intuitive response to potential danger:

When it comes to danger, intuition is always right in at
least two ways:

1.   It is always in response to something.
2.   It always has your best interest at heart...

Clearly, not everything we predict will come to pass, but
since intuition is always in response to something, rather
than making a fast effort to explain it away or deny the
possible hazard, we are wiser (and more true to nature) if
we make an effort to identify the hazard, if it exists. If there
is no hazard, we have lost nothing and have added a new
distinction to our intuition, so that it might not sound the
alarm again in the same situation.[2]

The intuitive signal of fear invites us to think and then act in
ways that will help us avoid the danger, if there is danger ahead.
It should not cause us to panic. De Becker continues:

"The very fact that you fear something is solid evidence
that it is not happening. Fear summons powerful predictive
resources that tell us what might come next. It is that which
might come next that we fear—what might happen, not
what is happening now...

What you fear is rarely what you think you fear—it
is what you link to fear. Take anything about which you
have ever felt profound fear and link it to each of the
possible outcomes. When it is real fear, it will either be
in the presence of danger, or it will link to pain or death.
When we get a fear signal, our intuition has already made
many connections. To best respond, bring the links into

---

[1]Miriam Greenspan, *Healing Through the Dark Emotions: The Wisdom of Grief, Fear, and Despair* (Boston & London: Shambhala, 2004), 170.
[2]Gavin de Becker, *The Gift of Fear* (New York: Dell, 1997), 82.

consciousness and follow them to their high-stakes destination— if they lead there.[3]

This discipline of linking the fear to the high-stakes or worst-
case destination does three things:
1. It helps us determine whether the danger is imminent and
therefore requires immediate action. For example, my fear of
heights is linked to the physical danger of slipping and falling thirty
stories, which is then linked to the fear of ending up smashed on
the pavement below. It takes two links to death. No wonder my
heart rate went up, my system went into higher alert, and I therefore
proceeded with greater caution—checking the balcony floor to
make sure it was not slippery and making sure that the railing was
solidly built—before I leaned on it. Was I overly cautious? Perhaps.
But the bottom line was: I did not trust the railing, the balcony, or
the building because I was unfamiliar with it. My fear, which led
to my cautious behavior, was justified.
2. Linking a fear to its most terrible destination helps us discern
an unwarranted fear and therefore alleviate the anxiety that may
be triggered by the fear. For example, if I have a fear of speaking
in public, this fear could be linked to the fear of being perceived
by my audience as incompetent. This would get back to my boss,
and she would fire me. Without a job, I would not be able to pay
the mortgage of my home or provide for my family and loved
ones. My family would reject me. I would be homeless and alone.
I would be perceived by others as useless and a burden to society. I
might die of hunger or catch some nasty disease. I would not have
insurance to pay for my needed care, and I would die. Although I
may link the fear of public speaking to death, I can also see that it
would be a long and unlikely trip. Linking fear to its most terrible
destination helps us distinguish between fear signals that predict
real danger and the fears that are not warranted. [4]
3. When we are able to link a fear to its ultimate horrible
destination, we can begin to see the fear in its wider context. This
is like "going on a train ride' of inquiry: probing the depths of
your fear to the final stop or destination, and then widening fear's
story from this end point."[5] Let me continue with my example
of my fear of speaking in public. I took the long train ride and

---

[3]Ibid., 341–42.
[4]Ibid., 342–43.
[5]Greenspan, *Healing*, 199.

arrived at the final destination, which is death. Now, I knew that it was unlikely that I would die from speaking in public; however, I needed to ask myself: what was the wider story emerging out of this fear? Perhaps it has something to do with me not trusting my own ability—a lack of self-esteem. This one is easy to deal with. I may take a public-speaking class and learn the skills and techniques to give good speeches and be prepared when I am invited to speak in the future. But there is something deeper in this story of fear. It may have something to do with the fear of being rejected by a community. This is linked to my need for a community that accepts me. But doesn't everybody need to have a loving accepting community independent of one's ability to perform? This wider context of this fear caused me to spend my time and energy to learn how to develop affirming, accepting communities not just for myself but for others as well. By pondering the wider story of this fear of public speaking, I discovered an area in my personal life about which I can do something to improve. I also discovered a greater need of others, which then becomes a call to the ministry to develop inclusive communities.

Taking the time to ponder my fear often points to opportunities for ministry. My fear of heights is linked to my fear of falling, which is linked to my fear of dying from hitting the ground. Having done all the cautionary steps to make sure that I am safe from falling, I need to ask myself: What is this fear of falling about? It probably has something to do with losing control, getting hurt, and dying. Now, I have some choices: I can avoid tall buildings, or I can meditate on my fear of uncertainty, loss of control, and death. Avoiding high places only limits the way I live—for example, missing the magnificent view on the mountains on the thirtieth floor balcony. Also, avoiding tall buildings will not help me live longer.

The other choice would be more productive: meditating on my fear of uncertainty, loss of control, and death. My fear of heights informed me that I'm afraid of death, which is a given in life. It tells me that no matter how hard I try to control things around me, they are not going to be totally in my control. This fear is asking me to live my life in the midst of things that I have no control over, and to live it knowing death is going to come. These topics are worth taking time to explore. As I ponder further on this direction, I may realize that the fear of chaos and death is a common experience among many people in the world in which we live. This exploration may lead me to enter a ministry to help people facing the end-stages of their lives. It may direct my attention and energy in creating a safer environment—working to provide more secure and safe jobs, finding ways to insure everyone has adequate healthcare, providing law enforcement organizations that respect the people they protect, etc.[6]

Fear and Phobias

If fear is such a good thing that could point us toward doing needed ministries, why do we have so much trouble dealing with it? Why did I have trouble admitting that I have a fear of heights? Why do people have phobias about so many things? Why do people do irresponsible things, putting themselves and others in danger, just to prove that they have no fear? To reap the fruit of fear requires us to face it head on. It requires the willingness to take that train ride to get to the last stop. However, the emotions and physical responses associated with fear are not something that I enjoy. Even when I have worked through a fear, in the end I would say to myself: "I never want to feel that again!"

Yet if we start avoiding fear itself, that is the beginning of our trouble with dealing with fear. It's not fear but avoiding fear that leads to phobias. Because we are scared to feel fear, we avoid whatever triggers it. It's the avoidance that locks the phobia in place. Phobias are one result of fear when its energy is toxified by avoidance...It's the fear of feeling the fear that stops you. If you can feel it, you can heal it...The raw emotion of fear itself is actually not paralyzing but energizing. Fear moves us to act—and if we avoid instead, the fear only grows.[7]

In the late 1980s, I was working as a campus minister at the University of Southern California. One of my students, David, came to my office and told me that he had been diagnosed with a rare form of cancer. In a week, he was hospitalized and then was pronounced as having AIDS. To put this in context, three months before, I presided at a funeral for a graduate student who died of AIDS. I did the funeral because his friends could not find anyone who would do it. I felt the sadness and the pain of his friends and colleagues, but I did not know him personally. Therefore, I was able to maintain a distance from all the emotions surrounding the passing of this young man. It was, however, different with David

---

[6]Ibid., 199–201. Greenspan has a similar exploration from fear of falling to finding purposeful actions to improve life around us.

[7]Ibid., 173.

because I had known him for over two years. AIDS was hitting closer to home this time.

The first time I visited him in the hospital, I sat and spoke with him for a long time. Before I left, I held his hands and we prayed. After I left his room, I immediately went to the bathroom. I washed my hands three times, looked up, saw myself in the mirror, and felt shame. During this time, little was known about the disease and how it was transmitted. My fear, which drove me to wash my hands repeatedly, was perhaps justified. Since so little was known about AIDS, I made the link that if I contracted AIDS by touching him, I might soon die from one of those rare diseases.

As more research on AIDS was done and the results made known to the public, I learned that AIDS was caused by the HIV virus. The only way one could contract the HIV virus was by exchanging bodily fluids, especially through the bloodstream. After I learned that, I had no fear of touching people with AIDS.

Even with the helpful knowledge I gained from the most up-to-date AIDS research, I still felt helpless as I watched David withering away. He died three months after he came to my office to tell me he was sick. I felt incompetent as I tried to comfort David's partner and his family at the funeral. The pain of losing a young bright energetic student was a new and almost unbearable sensation. I was a campus minister in a college working with young people at the beginning of their lives; I was not supposed to watch young students dying and to preside at their funerals.

Three months after David died, his partner called and left a message on my office answering machine. I listened to the message with dread. Sure enough, he too was diagnosed as having AIDS. I erased the message; I never wanted to feel the shame, hurt, guilt, and loss again. I justified my action by saying to myself that he was not a student and I did not have any responsibility toward him. The shame and guilt of not returning his call continued to bother me, but I did not want to deal with it. I attempted to shut my feelings down. I did not want to talk about it with anyone, fearing that others might judge me for not having the courage to conquer my fear. I was on the edge of developing a phobia toward people with AIDS.

I could have continued to avoid the fear of AIDS by avoiding having anything to do with the subject. I could have stopped reading any new information about AIDS. But the less I knew, the more I would be fearful of it. I could have continued to avoid dealing people with AIDS. I remember seeing someone with sunken cheeks and an unnaturally dark complexion at the market, and I turned and walked down another aisle to avoid having to see this person face-to-face. The less contact I had with people with AIDS, the more fearful I would be the next time I encountered another person with AIDS. I could have continued to avoid having any discussions with anyone about AIDS. This avoidance could further alienate me from my colleagues and my friends. I could have continued to avoid dealing with my personal feelings of guilt, anger, and loss by shutting down that part of myself. But the less I knew about how I would react, the more afraid I would be to allow these feelings to be triggered. A phobia—any kind of phobia—inevitably alienates one from oneself and others, creating barriers that one would not want to cross because of the fear of feeling fear.

I was lucky to have friends around me who reached out to me and helped me break out of my potential phobia. The community at the campus ministry, which consisted mostly of students, wanted to know more about AIDS and how Christian spirituality addressed this looming epidemic. We worked together and created a series of workshops on the subject. Our workshop leaders were people who had done a lot of work with AIDS from medical, social science, and religious perspectives. In one of the workshops, a priest who had worked extensively with AIDS patients brought with him a person with AIDS. The two of them guided us in a meditation to get in touch with the experience of a person with AIDS, in the form of the Stations of the Cross. In this meditation, we walked with a person with AIDS as he connected his experience with Christ's suffering and dying on the cross. I came face-to-face with a person with AIDS while having to acknowledge Christ in that person. Through these programs, I worked my way out of my potential phobia by gaining more knowledge of the disease. I slowly regained the trust in my ability to face this fear. I did this in the midst of a trusting community with which I could share my innermost feeling—my fear. More importantly, we did this in the context of our relationship with God through Christ.

Avoiding Fear: Sexuality

Having fear is not the problem. Fear simply calls us to pay attention to potential danger. It could energize us to act to help ourselves and others to avoid the potential danger. The fear of fear is the issue, because it creates a phobia. As we avoid the feeling of fear, we avoid knowing the vulnerable part of ourselves. The less we know about the vulnerable part of ourselves, the less we are able to connect with others as a whole person. We would not want to enter into a relationship that would risk exposing that vulnerable part of ourselves. Phobia creates a distance between people, destroying any possibility toward intimacy.

For the last thirty years, the major Protestant denominations have had fierce debates about homosexuality. My reflection on that matter is not that some people are homophobic, but that a wider issue is at work. The issue is that we are sex-phobic.

"How many of you have actually had a conversation about sex and spirituality in your church?" I asked this question at the beginning of a dialogue workshop on sexuality and spirituality. Usually in a group of about fifty people, only three or four persons would raise their hands. The avoidance of talking about sexuality creates a phobia about the subject of sex. Why do we have such a phobia toward this basic part of human life? To answer this question, we first need to explore why we have a fear of sex.

Ernest Becker in his Pulitzer-Prize–winning book *The Denial of Death* wrote:

> Sexuality is inseparable from our existential paradox, the dualism of human nature. The person is both a self and a body, and from the beginning there is the confusion about where "he" really "is"—in the symbolic inner self or in the physical body...The inner self represents the freedom of thought, imagination, and the infinite reach of symbolism. The body represents determinism and boundness. The child gradually learns that his freedom as a unique being is dragged back by the body and its appendages, which dictate "what" he is. This is why it is so difficult to have sex without guilt: guilt is there because the body casts a shadow on the person's inner freedom, his "real self" that—through the act of sex—is being forced into a standardized, mechanical, biological role. Even worse, the inner self is not even being called into consideration at all; the body takes over completely for the total person, and this kind of guilt makes the inner self shrink and threaten to disappear.[8]

[8]Ernest Becker, *The Denial of Death* (New York: The Free Press, 1973), 41–42.

We are fearful of sex because it has a direct link to the loss of a major part of our identity—the symbolic inner self. The loss of this part of oneself during the sexual act can be experienced as a temporary death of that part of oneself. Therefore, our fear of sex is directly linked to our fear of death.

For generations, many communities dealt with the fear of sex by prescribing a set of rules and rituals surrounding it. These rules and rituals were there to help us deal constructively with this fear. For example, the contract of marriage made with mutual love assures that the couple can be vulnerable with each other in the sexual act and still maintain the trust that they will not negate each as simply the physical being. Ernest Becker said, "Love... allows the collapse of the individual into the animal dimension without fear and guilt, but instead with trust and assurance that his distinctive inner freedom will not be negated by an animal surrender."[9]

In the twenty-first century, many rituals and rules are tied to our use of technology. The use of a technology called a condom can be seen as a new rule and ritual that we employ to make sure that we will not let the physical side of ourselves take over completely, but will also take into account the well-being of our partners.

But most often, the rules and rituals became ways people avoid having to deal with the fear of sex. I was invited to a friend's family gathering. His cousin has a ten-year-old child, who was eating his dessert at the table. As the adults talked freely amongst each other, the word sex was used. The mother of the child gave a dirty look at the offender. A silent scream entered our ears: We're not supposed to talk about sex in front of the kid!

This avoidance is often enforced in the name of "protecting the children." However, I speculate that the avoidance is more about the adults' fear of the subject of sex. I am not advocating that we talk freely about sex with our children. I am inviting the readers to explore how we can communicate this basic part of being human in ways that don't turn it into a phobia. Most of us, while we were growing up, picked up the signal that sex was a forbidden subject. Even among adults, sex is often a topic to be avoided. The less we talk about it, the less we know about the subject, and the fear increases—which causes us to create more rules and rituals to avoid the subject even more, which in turn causes us to know less

---

[9]Ibid., 42.

and less about the subject. Meanwhile, we still yearn to know more about such a basic part of human life.

Then there are the abundant supplies of R-rated and X-rated movies, which show only the physical aspect of sex, with no respect for the spiritual inner self of the partners. This is why pornography is such a threat to many and why we are fearful of it because it actually shows the death of the spiritual inner self. For the same reason, many people fear the medical innovation of contraception and sexual enhancement drugs, because these medical technologies are perceived as focusing only on the physical aspect of sex.

When I went to college at the age of seventeen, I had not had a single conversation with anyone about sexuality at all. My knowledge of sex came from sneaking into R-rated movies and, later, watching X-rated movies at my fraternity. Even in that kind of all-male environment, nobody talked about sex in any meaningful way. We might as well have been watching these explicit sexual acts as isolated individuals. We had a yearning to know more about sex, but we were fearful of having real conversation about it. So we watched these movies and then felt guilty afterward. But the yearning to know did not go away.

Dealing with Sexuality

I was blessed with a campus minister who was not afraid to deal with sexuality as it relates to our spirituality. I remember that in one of the Bible study sessions in my third year in college, he surprised us—faculty, staff, graduate students, undergraduate students, and spouses—by engaging in an open dialogue about sex. Instinctively, he knew that if he had told us that we were going to talk about sex, we would act according to our phobia and shy away from attending. I had to admit that I and a few others were more than a little embarrassed. I remember that at the end of that dialogue session, I felt a real sense of community. This sense of community came from the established trust through which I felt I could be vulnerable and tell the truth of what I knew and did not know about the topic. The phobia that was imposed on me was broken, and real intimacy was achieved by facing this fear. In my case, the phobia was ambushed into a discussion on this forbidden subject.

At another dialogue session on sexuality and spirituality, we explored how humankind, beyond our physical bodies, had minds that could think great thoughts and spirits that could create new things. We were made in the image of God with many divine attributes. This creative part of ourselves sometimes went too far, and we began to think that we were gods ourselves. But sex reminded us, in no uncertain terms, that we were tied to our bodies, which were tied to pain, aging, and decay. We could do nothing about this decay of the body, which eventually leads to death. We concluded that sex humbled humankind into realizing that we were just human and not God.

You might ask, How did we get from talking about sex to the subject of idolatry? This has been a recurring experience—facing our fear and breaking out of our phobia can lead us to surprising new places. If we are willing and able to face our fear, we can move into exciting exploration of our lives in relationship with ourselves, others, and God.

The tragedy of AIDS had a positive effect, because it opened up a dialogue about sex on most college campuses in the form of talks about safer sex. The challenge of the gay, lesbian, bisexual, and transgender community to the church is not just about gaining acceptance but instead is a challenge to the church community to deal with its fundamental fear of sex itself. If we are to move through these challenges constructively and faithfully, we must treat them as opportunities for the community to explore and undo a collective phobia about a fundamental aspect of human life. If we are able to face this together, we might discover a new arena of ministries that enable people to develop ways to value both the physical and spiritual aspect of their relationship. We might discover a ministry that guides people to achieve real intimacy in a world of fear.

Facing Our Fears

Having fear is not the problem. Avoiding fear is. To reap from fear the fruit of ministry, we must learn to face our fear by following it, probing it, tracing it, and linking it to the most terrible destinations—usually meaning those involving pain, suffering, chaos, isolation, and death. Only then can we see the wider vision of what this fear is calling us to do.

From the time Jesus was betrayed, all of the male disciples of Jesus were nowhere to be found. They were hiding because of their fear. They were avoiding being perceived as having anything to do with Jesus, as evidenced by Peter's denial of Jesus three times. Not only were they fearful; they were avoiding fear, distancing themselves from Jesus—now a symbol of rejection, loss, suffering, pain, and possibly death.

But not the women.

> Many women were there, watching from a distance. They
> had followed Jesus from Galilee to care for his needs.
> Among them were Mary Magdalene, Mary the mother of
> James and Joseph, and the mother of Zebedee's sons. (Mt.
> 27:55–56, NIV)

The women followed Jesus from Galilee to Jerusalem and witnessed all the things that had happened. They were there, in spite of their fear, witnessing Jesus' ministry that led him to the ultimate terrible destination of death. In both Matthew and Mark's gospels, they were portrayed as watching Jesus dying on the cross from a distance. In John's gospel, the three Marys were even closer. "Near the cross of Jesus were his mother, and his mother's sister, Mary the wife of Clopas, and Mary Magdalene" (Jn. 19:25).

They were there, sharing the pain and suffering, grieving their loss, expressing their emotions in the open. They were there with Jesus to his final breath. They were there when the Romans took Jesus down from the cross. They were there when Jesus was entombed. But this was not the end of the story. "After the Sabbath, at dawn on the first day of the week, Mary Magdalene and the other Mary went to look at the tomb" (Mt. 28:1, NIV).

The Sabbath was a time to recollect oneself and reconnect with God. I am sure that the women did that. They might have pondered on the wider implication of the story of Jesus that they had witnessed. What did all this mean? Perhaps they went back to the tomb out of a sense of duty. Perhaps they went back ready to accept the final defeat—that Jesus was dead—and that their greatest fear had come true. Nevertheless, they went back. In their willingness to face this final destination, they discovered something unexpected!

> The angel said to the women, "Do not be afraid, for I know
> that you are looking for Jesus, who was crucified. He is not
> here; he has risen, just as he said. Come and see the place
> where he lay. Then go quickly and tell his disciples: 'He
> has risen from the dead and is going ahead of you into
> Galilee. There you will see him.' Now I have told you."
> So the women hurried away from the tomb, afraid yet
> filled with joy, and ran to tell his disciples. (Mt. 28:5–8,
> NIV)

The women were still afraid, but something was different: they were filled with joy. They headed back to Galilee, where they had started the journey with Jesus years ago. Their courage to face their fear to its final destination moves them beyond death—their most dreaded fear. There, they receive a call to go home, where they would start the journey again with renewed energy, and vision for ministry.

The story of Jesus as recorded in the four gospels in the Bible provides the linkages, the train ride, in taking our fear to its ultimate destination—death. There, we are invited to open ourselves to the resurrection—to go home and accept our responsibilities as disciples of Jesus; to name our fear, to face our fear, to live through our fear, to have compassion on others who are fearful, and to say to them what the angel said to the women at the empty tomb, what Jesus said to his friends when he appeared to them after his resurrection: Do not be afraid.

"Do not be afraid; I am the first and the last, and the living one. I was dead, and see, I am alive forever and ever; and I have the keys of Death and of Hades." (Rev. 1:17b–18)

Questions and Activities

1. Name a fear that you have and link it, step-by-step, to its dreaded destination—death.
   a. How many links did it take to get to death?
   b. What did you notice as you did the linking exercise?
   c. Does this fear truly signal imminent danger, meaning you need to do something about it right away?
   d. If this fear does not present any imminent danger, what would happen if you took time to reflect and explore what this fear is really about?
   e. How does this exercise help you see the wider picture of your fear?
2. When and how does a fear become a phobia? What can you do to stop a fear from becoming a phobia?
3. Describe a fear that has alienated you from others.
   a. What is the fear?
   b. Who are the ones from whom you are alienated?
   c. In what ways can you face your fear so that you can reconnect with the others?

4. Have you ever had a conversation on sex and sexuality in church?
    a. If yes, what was it like? Did it help you deal with any particular or general fear?
    b. If no, why do you believe your church has avoided talking about sex and sexuality, which are basic parts of being human?
5. What does it mean for you to face your fear? What would you gain from doing so? What would you lose?
6. How does the story of Jesus inform you about how to deal with your fears?

2

Fear, Marketers, Politicians, and Symbolic Substitutes

One night in June, 2006, in Los Angeles, I was watching the local evening news. The lineup of stories in the first ten minutes was as follows:

1. Two men were shot for no apparent reason in Anaheim. The reporter ended the story by saying some people were moving out of the neighborhood for fear of their safety.
2. A terrorist threat paralyzed Port Hueneme because someone wrote graffiti on one of the walls implying a threat to the President of the United States. The port was shut down for three hours. The report concluded with the statement that it was impossible to inspect all incoming cargo, so our ports are not safe from terrorist plots.
3. The weather was going to be hot and humid because of air filled with hot moisture from the south.
4. The drinking water in Gorman was declared clear of E. coli bacteria. The reporter ended by admitting that no one knew how the water got contaminated in the first place.
5. Next was the case of a missing boy who was last seen at his home. He went out to play, and two hours later was gone.
6. A man opened fire at a casino in Las Vegas, killing a man and wounding a woman. He escaped and was armed and dangerous.
7. A Navy pilot died in a plane crash.
8. Moose, the Jack Russell terrier who played Eddie the dog on the television show Frasier, died.
9. A father and a son turned themselves in to the police in San Fernando—this was happening live on TV. Earlier, the father told his son to get his gun. He shot the neighboring

family multiple times because he said his neighbors had been bothering him for years.

10. Our state faced a prison crisis. The governor announced that a major prison improvement was needed because we had 70,000 more inmates than the existing prisons were designed to accommodate.
11. Rush Limbaugh was charged with possessing the drug Viagra for which he did not have a prescription.
12. Summer storms dropped 17 inches of rain in three hours on the East Coast.
13. We, in California, were getting the moisture too. Monsoon flows from the south created hazy, hot, and humid weather. Everyone should be prepared for thunderstorms or showers.

Within ten minutes of watching the evening news, I discovered that people were killing people for no apparent reason; neighbors could come over and kill me simply because I bothered them; our neighborhoods were becoming more and more unsafe; my child could disappear if I let her out of my sight for a moment; there were more criminals than ever—look at our overcrowded prisons; our ports were not secure, and terrorists could be lurking around them; flying on a plane could be dangerous because even experts like a Navy pilot could crash a plane; our water could be unsafe, and we don't know why; and finally, we have no control over our weather—remember Hurricane Katrina, which destroyed New Orleans in 2005? This could happen in New York or even at home in California. Then, in the midst of all the projections of fear, what were we supposed to do with the passing away of Eddie, the actor-dog, and Rush Limbaugh's erectile dysfunction?

Reacting to Fear, Not Love

Richard Nixon said, "People react to fear, not love. They don't teach that in Sunday school, but it's true."[1] Barry Glassner, the author of *The Culture of Fear,* further asserted that this "principle, which guided the late president's political strategy throughout his career, is the sine qua non of contemporary political campaigning. Marketers of products and services ranging from car alarms to TV news programs have taken it to heart as well."[2] Indeed, "immense

---

[1]Cited in Barry Glassner, *The Culture of Fear* (New York: Basic Books, 1999), xxviii. Glassner cited the Nixon quote from William Safire, *Before the Fall* (New York: Doubleday, 1975), Prologue.

[2]Glassner, *Culture of Fear,* xxviii.

power and money await those who tap into our moral insecurities and supply us with symbolic substitutes."[3]

Nixon was right in saying that fear gets our attention. Fear, as an intuitive response to potential danger, alerts us physically and emotionally to help us to survive. Marketers, politicians, and the news media want our attention. To get our attention, they evoke fear in consumers, voters, or their targeted audience.

The evening news wants us to stay tuned and watch, so in the first few minutes of the programs, the headlines are jam-packed with stories that evoke the most fear in us—fear of our neighbors, fear of the environment, fear of terrorists, fear for our loved ones, fear for our safety, etc. "Local news rarely provides new or relevant information about safety, but its urgent delivery mimics importance and thus gets our attention, much as someone would if they bust into your home and yelled, Don't go outside, or you'll be killed! Listen to me to save your life!' That's the way local television news works as a business. Fear has a rightful place in our lives, but it isn't the marketplace."[4]

Marketing and Fear

Back to that June evening: after the first ten minutes of terror-filled headlines, I was treated to commercials telling me that if I drank a certain drink or used a certain hygiene product, I would overcome my fear of rejection by a boy or a girl I adored. I was told that if I bought certain equipment or services, I would not be afraid of getting lost or being attacked or invaded by criminals. News, as presented through our television stations, works hand-in-hand with the marketers of products. The news gets our attention with projections of fear—of which some are real and we should pay attention to, but most of which are manufactured to get our attention; and then products—symbolic substitutes—are sold to us that promise to provide safety and ways to overcome our fears.

This principle of projecting fear to get our attention works also with so-called entertainment programs. Take a look at many of the popular television shows in the year 2006: *Law and Order, Medium, Close to Home, Without a Trace,* and *CSI* all begin with a crime that evokes fear to get our attention. The message could be: this crime could happen to you, so watch this program to find out more. Even comedies such as Desperate Housewives build into their

---

[3]Ibid.
[4]Gavin de Becker, *The Gift of Fear* (New York: Dell, 1997), 358.

storylines fear-evoking crimes—who knows, your neighbors could be killers and kidnappers. Of course, the more popular the show, the more the marketers want to buy commercial time during the show to sell their products.

Politicians and Fear

Politicians have also learned to use fear to get our attention. In the May 2006 issue of *Vanity Fair* magazine, Al Gore wrote an article called "The Moment of Truth," warning the readers about the dangerous effects of global warming and how we must act quickly to reverse the dangerous trend. Here are direct quotes from the article:

> "The voluminous evidence suggests strongly that, unless we act boldly and quickly to deal with the causes of global warming, our world will likely experience a string of catastrophes, including deadlier Hurricane Katrinas in both the Atlantic and the Pacific."

> "We are melting virtually all of the mountain glaciers in the world...Polar bears are dying by drowning."

> "We are beginning to melt—and possibly de-stabilize—the enormous, 10,000-foot-thick mound of ice on top of Greenland and the equally enormous mass of ice in West Antarctica,...rais[ing] the sea level worldwide by more than 20 feet."

> "Global warming, together with the cutting and burning of forests and the destruction of other critical habitats, is causing the loss of living species at a rate comparable to that of the extinction of dinosaurs 65 million years ago."

> "The ocean is going to become so acidic that [it] makes it more difficult for many ocean creatures, large and tiny, to make shells, because the shells would instantly dissolve in the newly acid ocean water, the way chalk dissolves in vinegar."

> "All of this, incredibly, could be set in motion in the lifetime of children already living—unless we act boldly and quickly. Even more incredibly, some of the leading scientific experts are now telling us that without dramatic changes we are in grave danger of crossing a point of no return within the next 10 years!"

So far, the above scientific evidences were convincing, and they evoked fear to get my attention. Gore's intention was to get me to do something about global warming. The mention of Hurricane Katrina was justified because the unusually strong storm confirmed the scientific findings. I believe the scientific evidence that he presented, and I was ready to act on this real threat to my own safety, the wild animals, the sea creatures, and future generations. But then, Gore continued:

> For example, the administration was warned on August 6, 2001, of an attack by al-Qaeda. "Bin Laden Determined To Strike in US," said the intelligence community in a message so important that it was the headline of the president's daily briefing that day, five weeks before the attacks of September 11. Didn't he see that clear warning? Why were no questions asked, meetings called, evidence marshaled, clarifications sought?
>
> The Bible says, "Where there is no vision, the people perish."
>
> Four Augusts later, as Hurricane Katrina was roaring across the unusually warm water of the Gulf of Mexico and growing in to a deadly monster that was less than two days away from slamming into New Orleans, the Administration received another clear warning: the levees—which had been built to protect the city against smaller, less powerful hurricanes—were in grave danger. But once again an urgent warning was ignored. The videotapes of one session make clear that the president heard the warnings but, again, asked not a single question.
>
> Nearly 70 years ago, when a horrible and unprecedented storm of another kind was gathering in Europe, British Prime Minister Neville Chamberlain found it inconvenient to see the truth about the nature of the evil threat posed by the Nazis... [5]

Within two pages of this article, along with all the scientific research that pointed to the consequences and dangers of global warming, Gore evoked our related fears by linking global warming with Hurricane Katrina; September 11, 2001; the Nazis in World War II; the Bible; and the extinction of the dinosaurs.

With all the scientific data that he collected, why did Gore need to force the connections between global warming with the major fear-triggering events in our recent history? Did he think that

---

[5]Al Gore, "The Moment of Truth," *Vanity Fair* (May 2006): 170–72.

the only way to get our attention concerning global warming was to trigger our fears connected with the most fearful events in our lives? Was he doing this because the public is already conditioned to pay attention only when fear is evoked?

Of course, it is not fair to just pick on Gore on this. Many politicians use the same technique to get our attention—and, hopefully, our support and votes. The Bush administration evoked the fear instilled in everyone in the United States on September 11, 2001, to gain the public's support to invade Afghanistan, which had a proven direct connection with the terrorists who attacked the United States on that day. Then the same fear was evoked to justify the invasion of Iraq. When it became obvious that Iraq had no connection with the September 11 attacks, another fear was evoked—weapons of mass destruction. In the 1980s, the anti-nuclear arms movement had used the same technique of evoking fear to get people to pay attention to the destructive power of nuclear arms. The fear-evoking technique was so effective that it not only created a mass movement of protest, but blockbuster movies like the Terminator trilogy also portrayed the destructive power of nuclear arms—simultaneously making a lot of money while further reinforcing this fear in the public.

The fear of WMDs was evoked again to gain the public support regarding the invasion of Iraq. I remember the pivotal moment when Colin Powell made his plea to the United Nation's Security Council when he was certain that Saddam Hussein had WMDs. After the initial full-scale invasion, the military operation was declared a victory. But when no WMDs were found in Iraq, another fear was evoked—the fear of the dictator. The fear of a dictator evoked an even deeper fear. Many immigrants in the past and the present came to the United States to escape tyrannical dictatorships in their home countries. In many of the dialogues I have facilitated about the war in Iraq, many people have said that getting rid of a dictator like Saddam Hussein was worth the sacrifices that our soldiers have made.

Gavin de Becker said, "What you fear is rarely what you think you fear—it is what you link to fear."[6] Media and politicians have learned this well. Every time they want us to pay attention, buy their products, or support them politically, they link their competition, opponent, or enemy with the person, groups, or

---

[6]de Becker, *Gift of Fear,* 342.

events that have implanted profound fear in us. When the link is not obvious or cannot be found, they create it.

Some people have called Al Gore an alarmist, perhaps because of the fact that he began using fear-evoking techniques to get his point across. The same people who accuse Gore of spreading fear are advocates of another kind of research that concluded that the warming trend is really a weather cycle the earth is going through and so there is no need to overreact. On the June 7 broadcast of *CNN Headline News,* host Glenn Beck compared *An Inconvenient Truth,* a documentary film about Al Gore's campaign to raise awareness of global warming, to the Nazis. Beck dismissed many of the conclusions drawn from the documentary, stating, "When you take a little bit of truth and then you mix it with untruth, or your theory, that's where you get people to believe...It's like Hitler. Hitler said a little bit of truth, and then he mixed in and it's the Jews' fault.'"[7]

Hitler seems to be a favorite fearful character to call to mind whenever someone wants to discredit a political opponent. We don't like what Al Gore is saying, so we link him with Hitler. We don't like George W. Bush's policy, so we link him with Hitler. I wanted to know if this technique of linking our enemies or political opponents with Hitler is true. I did some research on the World Wide Web. I went to one of the most popular search engines, Google.com, at the end of August 2006. I did a search on the names "Al Gore" and "Hitler" together. This means the resulting entries contain the two names within the same paragraph, or at least the same Web page. The search resulted in 2,040,000 entries. I decided to do a search on the names "George W. Bush" and "Hitler" and discovered there were 7,330,000 entries. I then did a search with "John Kerry," the 2004 Democratic presidential candidate, and "Hitler" and I got 2,720,000 entries.

Who do we believe? Which one of these political figures is really more like Hitler and should be feared more?

I decided to try "Bin Laden"—a known terrorist responsible for the horrible attacks on September 11, 2001—and "Hitler" and found only 1,210,000 entries—about half of the entries linking Hitler with John Kerry or Al Gore and outnumbered nearly seven to one by entries linking Bush and Hitler. Who is more like Hitler now? Whom do we believe?

---

[7]Quoted widely online, including at http://mediamatters.org/ items/200606080005.

Then I tried a search on "9/11" and "Iraq" and yielded an astonishing 190,000,000 entries. Wait a minute—Iraq had nothing to do with the September 11, 2001, attacks! I wondered what I would get if I googled "9/11" and "Afghanistan," which is a nation that actually had something to do with the terrorist attacks. I found a disappointing 81,800,000 entries—less than half of the entries linking 9/11 with Iraq. I then tried "al-Qaeda" and "9/11" and again I was even more disappointed with only 7,730,000 entries—less than 5 percent of those when involving Iraq.

The research I did using Google.com was not scientific by any means, and indeed, many of the entries containing 9/11 and Iraq may have been sites pointing out that they were not related. But look at the disparity between the facts and the number of times people on the Internet mentioned these names and events in the same paragraph or page. The country with a proven connection with the defining fear-evoking event for Americans in the beginning of the twenty-first century got mentioned less than half the time as compared with the nation that had nothing to do with that event. What are the motives of the people who make the unproven link between Iraq and 9/11? Who benefits from making this fearful but unfounded link?

Joe Lieberman lost the Democratic primary in 2006 for the U.S. Senate seat to challenger Ned Lamont because of the changing attitude toward the war in Iraq, a war he supported. Then, at the beginning of August, 2006, British intelligence uncovered a terrorist plot that involved plans to blow up ten airliners heading for the United States. Lieberman immediately played "the terror card" in his campaign to run as an Independent candidate. "If we just pick up like Ned Lamont wants us to do," he warned a campaign crowd, "get out by a certain date, it will be taken as a tremendous victory by the same people who wanted to blow up these planes."[8] Soon after he played the terror card, polls showed that he was leading Lamont. The Republican Party also tried to capitalize on this news of the London terrorist plot. The Republican National Congressional Committee circulated a memo urging Republican candidates to jump on the week's headlines: "Recent event has reminded us that we continue to operate in a pivotal phase in the global war on terror," it read. "You should move to question

[8]Jonathan Darman, "A Hawk Stays Aloft," *Newsweek* (August 21/August 28, 2006): 28–29.

your opponent's commitment to the defeat of terror and...create a definitive contrast on this issue."[9]

Media and Fear

By the way, the cover of the particular issue of *Newsweek* in which I found the article about Joe Lieberman and the Republican Committee memo from above has the following headline and graphics: In extra-big print: "TERROR NOW." Under it is an airplane in flight, heading from west to east, reminiscent of the planes hitting the World Trade Center five years ago. Under the image of the plane is the subhead:

"A PLOT AGAINST AIRLINES,

BIN LADEN AT LARGE,

IRAQ IN FLAMES,

FIVE YEARS AFTER 9/11,

ARE WE ANY SAFER?

LESSONS OF A GLOBAL WAR."[10]

Not only were politicians playing the "terror card," Newsweek magazine played that fear card to the hilt on its cover. The news programs on our television play the fear card every night in our living rooms. The entertainment programs, even the comedies, are playing the terror card. The marketers, the news media, and the politicians constantly feed us with a feast of fears every hour and every day. For what? Who will gain from spreading fear? What groups or organizations will benefit from these fear tactics? What do they want from us?

Politicians evoke fear because they want us to give them power by voting for them. They want us to change the polling results and give them a higher approval rating. The news media use fear to keep us watching their news and buying their papers and magazines, which are supposed to give us helpful information. Instead, in between the fear-provoking reports and images, they bombard us with advertisements and commercials trying to sell us products. But does voting for a certain politician really help us deal with our fear? Will buying a certain product alleviate our fear? They are but symbolic substitutes for what really will help us address our fear.

---

[9]Ibid.
[10]Ibid., front cover.

Buying these substitutes gives only the feeling that we are doing something about our fear. They offer only illusions of safety. They are only temporary releases. The feeling of safety wears out quickly, and we crave the next substitute when our fear, which was never addressed, surfaces again thanks to marketers and politicians. These substitutes distract us from doing the things that will help us face our fear, work through it, and discover our call to ministry.

Jesus and Fear of God

When it was almost time for the Jewish Passover, Jesus went up to Jerusalem. In the temple courts he found men selling cattle, sheep and doves, and others sitting at tables exchanging money. So he made a whip out of cords, and drove all from the temple area, both sheep and cattle; he scattered the coins of the money changers and overturned their tables. To those who sold doves he said, "Get these out of here! How dare you turn my Father's house into a market!" (Jn. 2:13–16, NIV)

Why was Jesus so angry? Jesus was angry because they were selling substitutes for the real sacrifice and offering the God demanded.

All that first opens the womb is mine, all your male livestock, the firstborn of cow and sheep. The firstborn of a donkey you shall redeem with a lamb, or if you will not redeem it you shall break its neck. All the firstborn of your sons you shall redeem. No one shall appear before me empty-handed. (Ex. 34:19–20)

But if you cannot afford a sheep, you shall bring to the LORD, as your penalty for the sin that you have committed, two turtledoves or two pigeons, one for a sin offering and the other for a burnt offering...Thus the priest shall make atonement on your behalf for the sin that you have committed, and you shall be forgiven. (Lev. 5:7, 10b)

In those days, making an offering for the atonement of sins required a long preparation leading up to the moment of the offering at the temple—raising livestock, preserving the firstborn, knowing what animal could be used to redeem the more valuable animal, etc. It involved bringing the livestock to the temple.

Buying something in front of the temple was the shortcut that gave the appearance of one's contrition as one went through the ritual offering. There was no need to go through all the trouble of raising animals and bringing them to the temple; just buy a couple of doves, and your sins would be forgiven. By the way, that was the cheapest way to go. They followed the law, but they forgot the essence of the law. "No one shall appear before [God] empty-handed." They responded to the fear in the presence of God with only substitute and not the fruit of their labor.

> [God] sent redemption to his people;
> > he has commanded his covenant forever.
> Holy and awesome is his name.
> The fear of the Lord is the beginning of wisdom;
> > all those who practice it have a good understanding.
> > (Ps. 111:9–10)

The fear of God was intimately tied to following the covenant God made with Israel at Mount Sinai. But the fear of God was supposed to lead to wisdom and understanding. (See chapter 5.) Following of the ritual prescribed by the covenant was not simply a physical act. The outward action represented the inward experience of grace that led to transformation and renewal of one's life. Instead of working through their fear of God, recognizing the sins that they had committed, and yet realizing that through God's mercy and grace they were forgiven, they brought substitutes that only satisfied the law externally without doing all the work needed to move from the fear of God to forgiveness by God. The substitute offering made the ritual of atonement hollow and meaningless. Jesus was angry at the people in front of the temple for selling substitutes to people, giving them the illusion of a right relation with God while making a profit. Jesus knew that there is no substitute for the struggle in facing our fears, our shortcomings, and our mortality, and then realizing that God still loves us.

In the world we live in today, we are not taught to work through our fear of God, fear of others, and fear of nature, a process that leads us to offer ourselves for ministries. Instead, marketers, politicians, and the media are projecting fears while offering us symbolic substitutes for the struggles that are needed to work through our real fears. We are offered sheep, cattle, and doves that we did not raise for the purpose of thank-offerings to God. Since these easy substitutes do not really address the fears at hand, we end up fearing even more the next time this fear is evoked. More substitutes are offered for us to buy to alleviate our fears again. We become addicted to the substitutes. And, in time, we are willing to pay more for them—not just our money or our votes, but our freedom, our sense of personhood, our care for our community, our love for God.

Seeing through Symbolic Substitutes

How can we be like Jesus and see through the symbolic substitutes the marketers, the politicians, and the news media offer? How can we cleanse our hearts and minds so that we can approach fear with the proper offering that involves our work, our spirit, and our lives?

We begin by asking: Who benefits from evoking this fear in me? What is the message being put forth along with the evocation of this fear? Am I being ask to do something? What substitutes am I being asked to buy to give me the illusion of safety? Is someone or some group going to gain monetary and political power by this? Aren't they the sellers of cattle, sheep, and doves? Then, like Jesus, we must learn to drive them out of our minds, our hearts, and our souls. Then, maybe we can see the genuine cry for attention based on real fear to which we should pay attention—fear for one's well-being, fear for the safety and spiritual well-being of others and of our communities, and fear of the destruction of the earth. Only then can we face our fears and work through them with real emotion, real heart, and struggles, linking the fears to their ultimate destination and seeing the bigger vision of God's plan and acting upon it with passion, love, and faithfulness.

Questions and Activities

1. Watch the first fifteen minutes of any prime time news program, including the commercials.
   a. What fears were triggered? List them.
   b. Make a list of the things that the commercials were selling. What fears did they trigger and what symbolic substitutes were they selling?
2. Listen to a recent political speech. Many are readily available online.
   a. Name the fears that this speech evokes in you.

    b. What does this politician want you to think, do, or be by evoking these fears?

    c. What promise does this politician make in order to keep you safe?

    d. Who might benefit from what you are asked to accept and do, monetarily and politically? In other words, who stands to make money and/or gain more power?

3. How do you avoid buying (or buying into) symbolic substitutes to address your fear?

4. What effective and constructive strategies can you use to address the fears that are triggered by politicians and marketers?

3

Rituals, Rules, Technologies, and the Color-Coded Threat-Level System

The horrible events of September 11, 2001, not only destroyed buildings and killed a lot of people, they also destroyed the sense of entitled security of the population living in the United States. Many people experienced, for the first time, the fear of unexpected attacks, loss, and death. Immediately after September 11, the people of the United States employed many rituals, rules, and technologies to deal with their fear, both consciously and unconsciously, individually and collectively.[1]

Rituals and Fear

From the beginning of history, humankind has used rituals to address life's inherent uncertainties. Human communities have surrounded the most uncertain and fearful times in life—such as birth, sickness, marriage, and death—with rituals. Many rituals have actually enabled people to work through their fear and to discover both new ways to relate to others and new ministries. For example, in church, the liturgy every Sunday helps the community to reconnect with each other and with God. In the middle of the liturgy is a time to pray for oneself and for others—our community, the nation, and the world. We pray for the sick and those in need; we pray for those who have died. We have a time for confessing our sins in which we repent of our alienation from other people, and from God. Then comes a time for forgiveness, followed by the peace—a ritual of reconciliation reconnecting each person

---

[1] Using technology, rules, and rituals to avoid uncertainties in life was described by cultural anthropologist Geert Hofstede in *Culture's Consequences—International Differences in Work-Related Values,* abridged ed. (Beverly Hills, London, New Delhi: Sage Publications, 1987), 110–47.

with the community. Many rituals, such as baptism, confirmation, marriage, anointing of the sick, and funeral rites, actually enable families and communities to come together to support the ones who are experiencing fear associated with major life transitions. The constructive rituals that people employed surrounding the September 11 attacks included gathering together in churches, temples, mosques, and synagogues to pray for those who died and for their families. Many were mobilized to contribute money and other means to support the victims' families. Many children wrote letters of support to the firemen and volunteers who were working around the clock in the rescue and recovery efforts at the World Trade Center site. These rituals were helpful, because they helped people who were experiencing fear triggered by this event to connect with others—to achieve a kind of intimacy that could help people face their fear knowing that others cared and were actively doing something to support them. Through these rituals they were actually doing something constructive in helping them face their fears together.

However, many rituals only served to give people the illusion that they were in control. They were substitute rituals that did not help people face their fears and work through them. At worst, they enforced our instincts to avoid facing our fear. For example, the ritual of displaying the United States flag on our front porch, windows, cars, and even baby strollers might have made some of us feel like we were doing something about this horrible event, and it might have made us feel better about being "Americans," but it did not really help us deal with our fear. I know this because accompanying all the rituals around the flags were the judgments and suspicions experienced by those who did not display a flag somewhere visible on their homes: "Since they are not displaying a flag, they must be unpatriotic and anti-American." Worse: "They might be terrorists." This ritual did not help people connect with each other, but rather increased the alienation, separation, suspicion, and fear of others.

On September 20, 2001, the President of the United States addressed a joint session of Congress. He invited people to "to live your lives and hug your children," and "to uphold the values of America, and remember why so many have come here." A little later in the speech, he said,

> I ask your continued participation and confidence in the American economy. Terrorists attacked a symbol

of American prosperity. They did not touch its source. America is successful because of the hard work, and creativity, and enterprise of our people. These were the true strengths of our economy before September 11th, and they are our strengths today.[2]

Many heard this, myself included, as the invitation to continue our daily lives as "normal" and not give into what the terrorists wanted us to do—to change our lifestyles and limit our activities. Instead of dealing with our fear, many followed the ritual of "business as usual." If we changed our way of life, then the terrorists had won. Therefore we ignored our fear, buried it, and continued to practice our ritual of living life as usual. Be good and patriotic Americans, and support the economy—which, for most people, meant: "Go and buy something." As the war was waged and talk of the power and strength of our military escalated, the Hummer—a military vehicle now marketed as an SUV—was selling fast, moving out of the car lots into the streets of every community in the United States.

Did buying something actually help us deal with our fear of insecurity? No, but buying something made some of us feel better and gave us the illusion that we were doing something to address our fear—"Look, I supported the economy." The fact was, our perception of living in the United States permanently changed on September 11, 2001. We were forced to enter a period of uncertainty and fear, not knowing what life would be like in the United States if a terrorist group (which we had hardly heard of until the President announced its name to Congress on television) could bring down an American icon of capitalism and success. Living life as usual and being calm and resolute were not going to help us in this wilderness of uncertainty. Waving flags and judging our neighbors for not doing the same was not going to help us find the trust in ourselves and neighbors again. Buying a Hummer was not going to help us face our uncertainty and work through our fear.

Rules, Technologies, and Fears

Rules and technologies are two other ways that human communities have addressed their fears—in particular, to lessen the uncertainty created by other people's actions that could harm

---

[2]Text of speech available online at www.whitehouse.gov/news/releases/2001/09/20010911-16.html.

us. It is no accident that after 2001, the popularity of technology-based TV shows rose significantly. Unlike the always-popular medical shows, which tell stories of how our medical technologies can help people deal with uncertainty and fear created by illnesses and diseases, new shows like *CSI, CSI: Miami, CSI: New York, NCIS,* and *Bones* showed us how technologies were used to solve crimes. We, the people, were interested in these shows because we had a yearning to believe that our technologies would somehow give us some kind of safety and certainty—if not actually preventing the crimes against us, at least solving the crimes after they were committed. We got to see the "bad guys" get caught and punished for their crimes. Hence, these technology-based shows worked hand-in-hand with always-popular rule-based shows like *Law and Order* and its many mutations—*Law and Order: Special Victims Unit,* and *Law and Order: Criminal Intent.* The rules, the laws of the land, that we set up to govern people's behavior would make us feel safer, because the rules would deter the crime—and because our technologies would help us catch and punish people when they broke the law.

One way of applying rules and technologies as ways to address our fears evoked by the attacks of September 11, 2001, went like this: If we were afraid that someone would bring a weapon on board to hijack a plane and thereby use it as a bomb to crash it into a building, we created rules at the airport—every passenger had to go through security screening. We used our technology, in the form of X-ray screening machines, to see through our bags. We waved a wand around a person's body to detect metallic weapons that a person might be carrying. These new rules would eventually be accepted by most people and became rituals that we partook of when we traveled.

Rules and technologies, when used appropriately, can actually help people deal with their insecurity and fear. For example, the technology of the mobile phone helped many on the day of September 11 to stay in touch—friends and families could support each other by talking and sharing their sense of loss and fear. The technology of television gave us information that we needed—knowledge of what was happening helped lessen our fear of the unknown. Everyone knew soon after the second plane hit the World Trade Center that flights had been ordered to land and eventually that only four planes had been hijacked. The new airline security rules after the attacks, such as random searches of passengers, confiscation of any sharp objects before a passenger is allowed to board a plane (and, later on, making people take off their shoes so they could be X-rayed), were rules that might actually deter potential terrorists and therefore would lessen our fear.

Color Codes and Our Fears

The color-coded threat-level system created by the newly formed Department of Homeland Security was a system of rules and technology that was supposed to help the citizens of the United States address their fear of a terrorist attack. According to the official information published on the Department of Homeland Security's website, this system

> is used to communicate with public safety officials and the public at-large through a threat-based, color-coded system so that protective measures can be implemented to reduce the likelihood or impact of an attack. Raising the threat condition has economic, physical, and psychological effects on the nation; so, the Homeland Security Advisory System can place specific geographic regions or industry sectors on a higher alert status than other regions or industries, based on specific threat information.[3]

Code Green means a LOW RISK of terrorist attacks. Code Blue means a GUARDED RISK of terrorist attacks. Code Yellow means ELEVATED RISK. Code Orange means a HIGH RISK of terrorist attacks. Code Red means a SEVERE RISK of terrorist attacks. On August 22, 2006, a week and a half after the revelation of a terrorist plot against airliners heading for the United States from London, I checked the "Current Threat Level" on the Homeland Security website. It said:

> August 22, 2006 – The United States' threat level remains at Code Orange, or High for all domestic and international flights. The ban on liquids and gels in carry on baggage remains in full effect.
>
> The Transportation Security Administration (TSA) ban now includes the following prohibitions, with some limited exceptions:

---

[3]From the website of Homeland Security, http://www.dhs.gov/dhspublic/display?theme=29.

- small doses of liquid medications permitted
- removal of shoes now required
- low blood sugar treatments, including glucose gel for diabetics permitted
- clarifications include: aerosols prohibited, solid lipstick and baby food permitted

Travelers will continue to see an increase in visibility and use of canine detection teams. Random gate inspections and bag searches will continue.

Recommended Activities

All Americans, including those traveling in the transportation systems, should continue to be vigilant, take notice of their surroundings, and report suspicious items or activities to local authorities immediately.

Everybody should establish an emergency preparedness kit as well as a communications plan for themselves and their family, and stay informed about what to do during an emergency situation.[4]

These communications technologies and the new set of color-coded threat rules that illustrate a set of behaviors appropriate for a given threat level were supposed to help us deal with our fear of a terrorist attack by helping us to know both where to get information and what to do with that information. Except for the last sentence in the DHS plan, where we are reminded to "establish an emergency preparedness kit" and "a communications plan" to stay informed, the bulk of the alert message has to do with a prescribed set of rules. They do not help us deal with our real fear.

In both the Yellow and Orange Alerts, one of the prescribed behaviors is for people to "continue to be vigilant, take notice of their surroundings, and report suspicious items or activities to local authorities immediately." This could be interpreted by many to mean that we are supposed to be suspicious of others and even to spy on our neighbors. In the beginning of 2006, we found out that the U.S. government had a secret program to eavesdrop on its citizens. People might therefore get the message that we are supposed to do that too. This prescription of behavior not only does not help people address their fear, it increases our fear by creating division and distrust among people and communities.

---

[4]Ibid.

In the same vein, for about two years after September 11, 2001, people could not say anything negative about our government or the President, because they were afraid that others might consider them unpatriotic. There were new rules also about our décor: if you did not display your flag prominently around your house in this neighborhood, you might be seen as unpatriotic and could be a potential terrorist. These new rules, which became ritualized over time, polarized people by dividing them into those who were patriotic and those who were not; those who supported freedom and those who did not. These rules increased the barriers between friends, families, neighbors, and political parties. They served only to allow us to avoid facing our fears by transferring our fears through projecting them onto others.

Many rules and technologies, which eventually become rituals, create the illusion of safety, when in fact they do very little to actually keep us safer or help us in dealing with our fears. In the years after 2001, even with added TSA personnel and screening technologies at airports, periodically we were told that someone had gotten a gun or a knife through security again. We equipped our soldiers with the latest technologies in weaponry and invaded two countries—one to hunt down the terrorists who executed the September 11 attacks, and the other to get rid of a tyrant who might have weapons of mass destruction. Yet five years later, we were told that we were no safer than before September 11, 2001. The terrorist who instigated the attacks was still at large. The country from which we removed the tyrant was on the verge of civil war, with daily counts of deaths and destruction. We created a new organization with new rules: the Department of Homeland Security that was supposed to help keep our country safe. Five years into the establishment of this new organization, we were told that our ports were not secured, our water supplies were vulnerable, and our borders were wide open. And when a disaster of major proportions happened, like the destruction of much of New Orleans by Hurricane Katrina in 2005, FEMA (the Federal Emergency Management Agency, once independent but now subsumed under the aegis of the Department of Homeland Security) was slow to respond to help the victims.

Five years after September 11, 2001, I learned that I could not count on my own country to put the resources in the right places to make its people and communities safer. And the technologies and rules that our government employed to keep us safe did not guarantee my safety, nor did it reduce my fear. The London terrorist plot, revealed in the summer of 2006, showed us that the terrorists had found another way to bypass the detection of metal-based weapons by using liquid explosives instead. The use of technologies and rules to keep us safe is only temporary. Those who are determined to harm others will find new technologies to counter the technological approach to our safety. They will find new ways to evade the new rules that we have designed.

What I have learned is that using external approaches, such as rules, technologies, and rituals, to deal with our fear is often ineffective. As long as we were buying substitutes for facing our fears, such as using our tax money to wage wars, hiring people in new uniforms to check the passengers and their bags at the airports, and devising color-coded alert systems that encourage us to be suspicious of our neighbors, we will continue to feel fear's negative effects in alienating us from ourselves, from others, and from our communities. We have to find other ways to address our fears that will bring people together in a trusting community, so that we can face our fears faithfully and work through our fears constructively.

Community Creation and Fear

We need to create communities in which people can get to know each other in deeper, more profound ways. Instead of using rules only to control people's behavior, we need to find ground rules for people to form communities in which they can share honestly their fears and apprehensions without being judged or belittled. With the trust established in such communities, we can truly support each other in facing and working through our fears, thereby moving us toward discernment of our call to ministry.

Instead of using technologies to give us the illusion of safety, instead of using technologies to attack our enemies and spy on our citizens, we need to find and utilize technologies that truly connect people and form networks that keep us informed with truthful information. We need technologies that can help people support each other in times of uncertainty and insecurity.

Instead of following hollow, prescribed rituals that only make us feel better temporarily, we need to find rituals that are liturgies that enable people to gather around God, reminding ourselves that our ultimate security resides in God. Jesus showed us the way to move from fear to ministry by facing it, pondering it, and linking it to its most terrible destination. Only then can we see and experience resurrection—knowing what God is calling us to do.

I was doing a workshop for a group of church leaders who were members of a committee that addressed societal issues for a major Christian denomination. I assumed that addressing major issues of the day was not new to this group. This was the year 2006! I discovered, to my surprise, that the group had not openly addressed the Iraq war. The reason they gave was that every time the topic came up, people became emotional, judgmental, and people shut down. In other words, they had developed a phobia about the war. This phobia, I observed, was creating alienation among this group of Christians serving in the same ministry.

After the group agreed to uphold a set of Respectful Communication Guidelines,[5] I invited them to form groups of ten and study the lectionary gospel lesson of the upcoming Sunday.[6] After that, I invited them to engage in a very simple dialogue about the Iraq war. The question was: How does the Iraq war affect you, personally? After a moment of silence, each table group was invited to share using Mutual Invitation.[7] Forty-five minutes later, I gathered the whole group and asked, "How was that?" The responses were nothing short of amazing:

> "This is the first meaningful conversation I've had about the war in Iraq."

> "I was afraid that we would get into the old yelling match, but then I found that though we might have very different perspectives on the war, we also share many things in common."

---

[5] There are many different sets of guidelines for respectful communication. The one I designed, called "Respectful Communication Guidelines," is from Eric H. F. Law, *The Bush Was Blazing But Not Consumed* (St. Louis: Chalice Press, 1996), 86–87.

[6] The full Community Bible Study process is documented in Eric H. F. Law, *The Wolf Shall Dwell with the Lamb* (St. Louis: Chalice Press, 1993), 121–31. We used a simplified version of the process, which can be found at the website of the Kaleidoscope Institute for Competent Leadership in a Diverse Changing World, www.ladiocese.org/ki.

[7] Mutual Invitation is a key technique that we use for group work that ensures everyone in the group is included. See ibid., 79–88.

"I may not agree with what some people said, but I now understand where they are coming from. What a difference that makes!"

"We can talk about it now, instead of avoiding the subject. I missed my friends."

I then asked them: What caused them to be able to become closer to each other again even when dealing such a "hot topic"? Some shared that having agreed to the Respectful Communication Guidelines was very helpful. They knew that they would not replay old destructive behavior. Others said that it was crucial for them to know that the other members of the group were persons of faith who loved God as well, and by listening to them share their reflections on Holy Scripture, they found that this was so.

Our avoidance of the fear of being rejected stops us from being vulnerable and telling the truth about our feelings, perspectives, and experiences. This results in alienation and distancing from each other, destroying the possibility of intimacy. The solution is to rebuild the trust by agreeing to a set of ground rules for community building. In this case, the Respectful Communication Guidelines and the Mutual Invitation process included everyone in the dialogue and enabled people to listen to each other without debate. The other key practice or constructive ritual is to gather around the words of Holy Scripture, inviting each other to share their connections and experiences of God working in their lives.

The LORD is my light and my salvation;
> whom shall I fear?

The LORD is the stronghold of my life;
> of whom shall I be afraid?

> > (Ps. 27:1)

Fear is projected all around us these days—fear of terrorist attacks, natural disasters, mysterious diseases, increasing crime, risk in relationships, etc. We need to develop communities of trust in which relationship and intimacy can be reestablished. In that spirit, I want to propose an alternative color-coded threat-level system that does not focus on behavioral rules and rituals, but suggests ways for people to get together with their neighbors and develop trusting communities in which they can address their fear faithfully, leading to constructive actions. Here is what I came up with:

Code Green

In this time of LOW RISK, get to know your neighbors.

- Go to the regularly scheduled neighborhood meetings. If there is not one scheduled, get together with your neighbors and approach community organizations to start one.
- Visit your neighbors on your street and in your apartment buildings. Invite your neighbors over for tea or coffee or to have lunch or dinner. Discuss what to do to support each other in case of a terrorist attack or an emergency.
- If you belong to a faith community, join a group that meets regularly to share experience of God.

Code Blue

In this time of GUARDED RISK, gather at your place of worship or community center.

- Review the emergency procedures with your community. If there are not any in place, create them together.
- Test out the communications technologies to make sure they work in keeping people informed.
- Join a dialogue program with people and groups from a different religion and neighborhood. Share honestly about your feelings and listen to others' hopes, dreams, and fears. Discuss what to do to in case of a terrorist attack or an emergency.

Code Yellow

In this time of ELEVATED RISK, educational institutions and workplaces should gather people in their organizations.

- Invite people to dialogue about their fears and to create a network of support in case of a terrorist attack or other emergency. The gatherings should also help people get more familiar with their environment at work, at school, and at home in the neighborhood.
- Walk through the emergency procedures that the schools, communities, and workplaces have set up.
- Faith communities should invite people to worship services and liturgies that help people to connect with each other and reaffirm their relationship with God. Interfaith prayer services are especially important.

Code Orange

In this time of HIGH RISK, contact your networks of support established during the Code Green, Blue, and Yellow alert times.

- Attend meetings and gatherings that have been set up previously.
- Make contact with people through the technologies that have been set up.
- Assess if there is imminent danger for your community. If your community is in danger, activate the emergency plan. If not, stay and share honestly your feelings and listen to others' concerns.
- Pray together if appropriate.

Code Red

In this time of SEVERE RISK, gather together with your family, and, when possible, with your neighbors.

- Assess if there is imminent danger or harm for your family and neighbors. If there is a major threat to your family's and neighbors' safety, activate your emergency plan. If not, stay together and share honestly about your feelings and listens to others' concerns.
- Pray together if appropriate.

I think this kind of community–trust-based alternative alert system should be designed and made available to airlines, churches, families, hospitals, schools, workplaces, and community centers— any place where people gather. I experienced a glimpse of what such a system might look and feel like when I was on a plane one month after September 11, 2001, heading for New York City. The passengers did not just carry their belongings and baggage on board—they were bringing with them the tension and anxiety that had started early that morning when they were moving through the ordeals of getting through security. But no one was willing to talk about it, so we all silently settled into our seats. I had been randomly selected to be searched for the last three times I had flown (since September 11). That day was no exception. But I had resigned myself to the fact that I was going to be searched, and so I had prepared for that. Since this was the first time I had returned to

New York City after the attack, I was more concerned with what I was going to do or say to my mother when I saw her; she lived and worked about twenty blocks from what had been the World Trade Center. My mind was occupied with thoughts of what I was going to do when I gave my workshop on Congregational Development for members of a church in midtown Manhattan.

As the plane was moving, the flight attendants gave the safety instructions. I observed that the instructions were not helping us to lower our apprehension. The plane finally took off. The pilot, in what I assumed was his usual communication to the passengers, came on the loudspeakers. He said,

> I know this is a time when flying on a plane could be scary. But I want you to reach over to your neighbors on this plane and introduce yourselves. Get to know each other. Talk about your experiences getting onto this flight. Learn about your neighbors' experiences in the last month since 9/11. Talk about your family and loved ones. Welcome to this flight, relax, and enjoy meaningful conversations. We will be arriving in New York City in about four and a half hours.

I introduced myself to the person sitting next to me, who was a publisher of a magazine based in New York. Once we started talking, we could not stop. We talked for most of the flight. Apparently we needed to do that. I needed to connect with someone and to articulate my feelings, which had been bottled up until that moment. I needed to know that I could get to know a stranger and establish trust again. Together, we turned a potentially stressful experience into a time of constructive dialogue. When I arrived in New York City, as I approached the Lower East Side in a taxi, smelling the burned ashes and dust from the World Trade Center that was no more, I felt a little more prepared to face my friends, colleagues, and relatives who had lived through that terrible event.

Questions and Activities

1. Rituals
   a. What are the rituals you use to deal with your fear?
   b. What are the rituals you see others use to deal with their fear? At home? At work? In school? In the neighborhood? In the city/town? In the state and nation?

    c. Which ones of these rituals actually help/work to address your fears? How can you find ways to share them and enable others to learn these rituals to address fears together?

    d. Which ones of these rituals do not help and may actually be harmful? What can you to do to replace these rituals with ones that are helpful?

2. Technologies

    a. What technologies do you use to deal with your fear?

    b. What technologies do you see others use to deal with their fear? At home? At work? In school? In the neighborhood? In the city/town? In the state and nation?

    c. Which technologies actually help/work to address your fears? How can you find ways to share them and enable others to use these technologies to address fears together?

    d. Which technologies do not help and may actually be harmful? What can you to do to replace these technologies with the ones that are helpful?

3. Rules

    a. What rules do you use to deal with your fear?

    b. What are the rules you see others use to deal with their fear? At home? At work? In school? In the neighborhood? In the city/town? In the state and nation?

    c. Which ones of these rules actually help/work to address your fears? How can you find ways to share them and enable others to use these rules to address fears together?

    d. Which of these rules do not help and may actually be harmful? What can you to do to replace these rules with ones that are helpful?

4. Review the proposed alternative color-coded threat-level system.

    a. List the helpful technologies, rules, and rituals that are embedded in this alternative color-coded system.

    b. With the people in your network—churches and neighborhood organizations—what rituals, rules, and technologies will you add to the list?

    c. Gather people from your neighborhood and your church, and create together a similar system that would help the community address terrorist threats as well as being disaster-ready.

4

Fear-Conqueror, Fear-Bearer, and Fear-Miner

On July 22, 2003, Army Private Jessica Lynch received a hero's homecoming. Thousands of cheering residents in Elizabeth, West Virginia, lined the streets, waving flags and holding all kinds of welcoming signs. According to the news reports I read, she wore a crisply pressed green uniform decorated with the ribbons of the Bronze Star, the Purple Heart, and the POW medal that she received the day before. I had been following Lynch's story up to that point. How could I not? For weeks, every television news program had been bombarding the viewers with stories of how Lynch was taken prisoner when her army unit was ambushed after taking a wrong turn near Nasiriya in Iraq in March of that year. The humvee in which she was riding was hit with a rocket-propelled grenade and crashed at high speed into the rear of an army tractor-trailer. Eleven soldiers died. Five others were taken prisoner. Lynch was taken to a hospital in Nasiriya and treated by Iraqi doctors. Her injuries included three fractures in her left leg, multiple breaks in her right foot, a fractured disk in her back, a broken right upper arm, and lacerations on her head. She was rescued on April 1 when Special Operations forces entered the hospital and removed her, took her to a nearby helicopter, and then flew her to safety. Since the rescue, she had endured four months of painful rehabilitation before she could come home. Authorities said that Lynch could not recall details of her ordeal from the time she was ambushed until "an unspecified point during her captivity."[1]

By the time the media covered Lynch's triumphant homecoming, all the facts had more or less been settled and were pretty

[1]CNN report on July 22, 2003.

much as I have summarized above. However, the facts were not so clear during the weeks immediately after her rescue story broke. "Jessica Lynch: Media Myth-Making in the Iraq War," an article from the website Journalism.org chronicled the news media's coverage of her story as follows:[2]

The story breaks

April 1, 2003—An Associated Press story reports that Lynch has been rescued and says that an army spokesman "did not know whether Lynch had been wounded or when she might return to the United States."

The wounds become gunshot wounds

April 2—*The New York Times* runs a story on the celebrations in Lynch's hometown and reports that, "Details of what happened to Private Lynch were scarce. An Army official said Tuesday night that Private Lynch had been shot multiple times. The official said that it had not been determined whether she was shot during the rescue attempt or before it."

An Associated Press roundup story mentions Lynch in the final paragraphs. "Officials who spoke on condition of anonymity said she was suffering from broken legs, a broken arm, and at least one gunshot wound."

Lynch as female Rambo

April 3—The day after its initial story, *The Washington Post* runs a story, "'She Was Fighting to the Death'; Details Emerging of W. Va. Soldier's Capture and Rescue" that recounts Lynch's ordeal. The account is reprinted in other newspapers.

"Lynch, a 19-year-old supply clerk, continued firing at the Iraqis even after she sustained multiple gunshot wounds and watched several other soldiers in her unit die around her in fighting March 23, one official said."

Questions arise about her wounds

April 4—The Associated Press reports that doctors told Lynch's father "she had not been shot or stabbed during

---

[2]These summations of media reports are from the website www.journalism.org, which is the joint Internet presence of the Project for Excellence in Journalism and the Committee of Concerned Journalists.

her ordeal. 'We have heard and seen reports that she had multiple gunshot wounds and a knife stabbing. The doctor has not seen any of this,' Gregory Lynch Sr. said."

April 5—An AP story reports that there is mystery about how Lynch was injured, but deep in the piece says, "Lynch's family in West Virginia said doctors had determined she'd been shot. They found two entry and exit wounds 'consistent with low-velocity, small-caliber rounds,' said her mother, Deadra Lynch."

The story begins to grow
April 7—The April 14 *Newsweek* hits the stands. "The unpleasant implication was that she might have been shot after she'd been captured, rather than wounded in combat," *Newsweek* reports. The account also raises the possibility of mistreatment in the Iraqi hospital and quotes her father as saying "she survived for part of her time in the hospital on nothing but orange juice and crackers."

The questioning of what actually happened begins
April 15—*The Washington Post* runs a piece on page A17 that questions its earlier account. A physician from the Iraqi hospital that treated Lynch calls the rescue "a big show... There were no bullets or shrapnel or anything like that." At the hospital, he said, "She was given special care, more than the Iraqi patients."

April 27—The *St. Louis Post-Dispatch* runs a long piece looking at the stories that the media got wrong in Iraq, including a large section on Lynch:

"Key elements in the story appear to have been wrong. Lynch's father and her Army doctor have both said there is no evidence that she was shot or stabbed. There is as yet no substantiation of any torture. Doctors at the hospital say that when the rescue team swooped in, the building was undefended; militia forces had fled the day before."

The reconsideration of the story picks up steam
May 15—In a piece by a BBC reporter, the London daily *The Guardian* deconstructs the Lynch story in an 1,800 word story that calls her account "one of the most stunning pieces of news management yet conceived." The story

quoted several Iraqi sources who claimed that Lynch had not been shot or stabbed, that she received good care, that the U.S. military had been told the Iraqi paramilitary guards had left the hospital before the raid, and that two days before the raid the hospital had tried to return Lynch to U.S. forces nearby, but were fired upon and returned to the hospital.

May 19—On his website journalist Andrew Sullivan attacks the BBC piece in his blog. "Meanwhile, the latest BBC smear is against Private Jessica Lynch. Glenn has the goods. I remember the reporter, John Kampfner, from my Oxford days. He was an unreconstructed far-lefty. No doubt these days he's a reconstructed one."

June 17—In a lengthy front-page story, *The Washington Post* prints an investigation of its own April 3 story on Lynch. The new story finds:

"Lynch's story is far more complex and different than those initial reports...Lynch tried to fire her weapon, but it jammed, according to military officials familiar with the Army investigation. She did not kill any Iraqis. She was neither shot nor stabbed, they said...

"The Special Operations unit's full-scale rescue of the private, while justified given the uncertainty confronting U.S. forces as they entered the compound, ultimately was proven unnecessary. Iraqi combatants had left the hospital almost a day earlier, leaving Lynch in the hands of doctors and nurses who said they were eager to turn her over to Americans."

That afternoon, CNN airs stories that essentially recount the *Post's* story. "According to the accounts that are now coming to light at the Pentagon, Private First Class Jessica Lynch got some very decent medical attention from the Iraqi doctors at the hospital in An-Nasariyah, where she was taken...[I]t appears that all of her injuries were from that portion of the incident, that she did not suffer gunshot or stab wounds but rather very serious concussion fractures, if you will, from this incident."

In November, 2003, the book *I Am a Soldier, Too: The Jessica Lynch Story,* by Rick Bragg, was published by Alfred A. Knopf and put on sale on Veterans Day. In an article from *USA Today* (November 6, 2003) titled "Lynch book tells of rape by captors," Rick Hampson reported:

> In the book, author Rick Bragg writes that scars on Lynch's body and medical records indicate she was sodomized, but that Lynch recalls nothing: "Jessi lost three hours. She lost them in the snapping bones, in the crash of the Humvee, in the torment her enemies inflicted on her after she was pulled from it."
>
> He adds, "The records do not tell whether her captors assaulted her almost lifeless, broken body after she was lifted from the wreckage, or if they assaulted her and then broke her bones into splinters until she was almost dead."
>
> Lynch told ABC News' *Primetime* in an interview to be broadcast Tuesday night that, although she doesn't remember being assaulted, "Even just the thinking about that, that's too painful."
>
> In the book, Lynch admits she was no hero: "I didn't kill nobody." In the broadcast interview, ABC's Diane Sawyer asked her, "Did you go down, like somebody said, [like] Rambo?" Lynch replied, "No. No. I went down praying to my knees. And that's the last I remember."
>
> "I did nothing," she added. "I mean, I was just there in that spot, you know—the wrong place, the wrong time."

Fear-Conquerors and Fear-Bearers

The Jessica Lynch story revealed two primary images that the U.S. media consistently instilled in the public's minds on how to deal with fear—the fear-conqueror and the fear-bearer. In a period of six weeks, Lynch moved from being portrayed as a "female Rambo" to just a "victim and a survivor." In either case, she was hailed by many as a hero. At the time the story broke, the United States was less than two weeks into the war in Iraq. The media's coverage of the fighting had taken a negative turn. The nation was perhaps fearful of whether it was doing the right thing by invading Iraq, and was it able to do the necessary job that the President had proposed? To address this collective fear, the media presented the Jessica Lynch story first with the fear-conqueror image, but when the Rambo-like "facts" were being disputed and discredited, the media moved—first reluctantly, and then wholeheartedly—to depicting her as a victim who survived this ordeal—as the fear-bearer.

I borrow these terms from Miriam Greenspan, author of the book *Healing Through the Dark Emotions*. She used the term "fear-carrier." I prefer "fear-bearer," which is more descriptive of that approach to fear. While she used these terms to differentiate the way males and females typically have dealt with their fears, I choose to use these terms more generally, applying them to different groups in different communities. She wrote, "Fear-conquerors are symbolically linked to heroism and power. Fear-carriers are symbolically linked to victimization and powerlessness."[3] Fear-conquerors deal with fear through

> acts of aggression against an "other" seen as enemy. From the Pentagon to the Mafia, from the streets of the Middle East to the hallway of our high schools, unacceptable fear is conquered through various forms of organized aggression and violence...The pop culture hero is an armored male machine with no fear of injury or death, willing to risk anything to subdue or kill the enemy. His courage is not so much acting despite fear as acting without fear.[4]

Fear-bearers are taught to "embody vulnerability and fear more overtly." Fear is "not an enemy to be conquered but a warning tack that says: Go no further...If you're a [fear-bearer] and you don't use fear to limit yourself, there is an implicit threat of violence."[5] Even though Lynch consistently said she did not remember, the media's image-making machine insisted that something more terrible must have happened if she was not a fear-conqueror. She could not have just lain there and been taken care of by the enemy! She had to be tortured or raped, which would make the exaggerated heroic rescue more satisfying.

The projected images of Jessica Lynch in the media after her rescue fit these two archetypal approaches to fear. She was first a fear-conqueror—fearless and strong—and then she was a fear-bearer who had crossed the line and had terrible violence (also exaggerated) visited upon her. She was helpless and in need of rescue by the fear-conquerors—the team who rescued her. But she survived, and that was enough for us to call her a hero.

Neither approach sees any value in fear. "Fear is not mined

---

[3]Miriam Greenspan, *Healing Through the Dark Emotions* (Boston & London: Shambhala, 2004), 181.
[4]Ibid.
[5]Ibid., 182.

for its gifts; it's banished, numbed and acted out."[6] Both of these approaches avoid facing and working through fear, and have the potential of turning the fear into a phobia. When asked about her alleged assault, Lynch said, "Even just the thinking about that, that's too painful."

The U.S. Government and Fear-Conquerors

The reaction of the U.S. administration to the September 11, 2001, terrorist attacks was a fear-conqueror's response to fear. The administration immediately went into conqueror mode. Benjamin R. Barber, in his book, *Fear's Empire,* described this well:

> In the epoch-defining speech he gave at the National Cathedral a few days after 9/11, the president said, "We are here in the middle hour of our grief. But our responsibility to history is already clear: to answer these attacks and rid the world of evil." At the conclusion of his speech,... the congregation stood and sang "The Battle Hymn of Republic."[7]

Bathed in patriotic and religious rituals, new rules were being defined to justify aggression; later, the doctrine of preemptive strikes was born. Since we could not prevent the world from entering into our entitled safety boundary, we had to go out and conquer the world using our latest technology in weaponry. Day after day, we were shown through the ever-eager media how our soldiers, loaded with the latest gear, won battle after battle. As long as we were striking back, it did not matter who or how it was justified—we were conquering our fear.

We had the opportunity to rethink our actions and to help the people of the United States to deal with our continual fear of terrorism after we had been successful in the war in Afghanistan. Instead of using our resources to ensure that Afghanistan and the United States were safer from terrorist threats, the U.S. administration waged another war against another country. We had no idea how to face our fear except through the fear-conqueror's way of aggression. "Violence is often a direct consequence of denied fear, fear acted out because the person has lost the ability to feel it authentically and mindfully, and to express it without shame.

---

[6]Ibid.
[7]Benjamin R. Barber, *Fear's Empire* (New York & London: W.W. Norton & Co., 2003), 40.

People act out because they are afraid to feel, afraid to speak of their fear."[8]

U. S. Citizens as Fear-Bearers

On the other side of the equation, the everyday people of the United States were made to conform as fear-bearers. On September 20, 2001, President Bush addressed a joint session of Congress. After he identified the terrorist organization that instigated the attacks, and said that the United States was at war, he said:

Americans are asking: What is expected of us? I ask you to live your lives, and hug your children. I know many citizens have fears tonight, and I ask you to be calm and resolute, even in the face of a continuing threat.

I ask you to uphold the values of America, and remember why so many have come here. We are in a fight for our principles, and our first responsibility is to live by them. No one should be singled out for unfair treatment or unkind words because of their ethnic background or religious faith. (Applause.)

I ask you to continue to support the victims of this tragedy with your contributions. Those who want to give can go to a central source of information, libertyunites. org, to find the names of groups providing direct help in New York, Pennsylvania, and Virginia...

I ask for your patience, with the delays and inconveniences that may accompany tighter security; and for your patience in what will be a long struggle.

I ask your continued participation and confidence in the American economy. Terrorists attacked a symbol of American prosperity. They did not touch its source. America is successful because of the hard work, and creativity, and enterprise of our people. These were the true strengths of our economy before September 11th, and they are our strengths today. (Applause.)

And, finally, please continue praying for the victims of terror and their families, for those in uniform, and for our great country. Prayer has comforted us in sorrow, and will help strengthen us for the journey ahead.[9]

---

[8]Greenspan, *Healing*, 186.
[9]Text of speech available online at www.whitehouse.gov/news/releases/2001/09/20010911-16.html.

While the administration was planning to go to war—the heroic fear-conquerors' approach to fear—we, the people, were told to live our lives and hug our children. We were told to continue to participate in the American economy. We were told to pray. We were told to have patience in facing the inconveniences of tighter security when we traveled. In the months that followed, the call for patience for many came to mean: keep your mouths shut and endure the new rules that are being imposed on you in the name of security. For example, no one can make a joke about security in the airport. Certain types of people were being singled out and searched in the airport, even though the President said explicitly, "No one should be singled out for unfair treatment or unkind words because of their ethnic background or religious faith." The message that many were getting was: don't step beyond the new boundaries, or there will be consequences.

I was at Los Angeles International Airport a few months after September 11, 2001. Because of a flight cancellation, I had to run to another terminal to board another flight from another airline. This meant that I had to walk out of the secured area of the terminal and run to the other terminal, only to face going through all of the security rituals all over again. The difference is that I only had thirty minutes to do this.

I arrived at the designated terminal and was horrified to see a very long line of people waiting to get through security. I spotted a person who was directing people at the end of the line. I showed him my passport and my ticket. I was hoping that this person would help me get through security quicker. As he was reading my ticket, I pointed out to him that I now only had twenty minutes to get to my flight. He looked up at me, and without any expression, he directed me to the shorter of two queues winding their ways to the screening booths.

I thought to myself, "Good, he was directing me to the quicker line." After standing in the line for a minute or so, I realized that the line I was in was not moving, while the other line was slowly, but consistently, moving. I looked at the queue of people snaking in front of me and the new ones that had just joined the line behind me; a sinking feeling came over me. I was in a special line where everyone was being searched.

The person who heard my plea for help did not help me; instead, he was punishing me for breaking the rules. I took a minute to calm down. I said to myself: What is the worst thing that could happen? I would miss my flight, in which case I would get another one. Finally, the line I was in moved a little bit, and I was at a position where I could scan the other people standing in my line.

Out of twenty-five people, at least fifteen were persons of color. As I listened to the conversations, most of the people of European backgrounds on this line spoke with a non-U.S. accent when they spoke English. Some spoke other European languages. My line moved a little more, and I edged closer and closer to the screening machines. I looked beyond and saw a security person waving a metal-detecting wand around an African American boy of no more than twelve years of age while his father was waiting impatiently and silently for him at the far corner of the room.

My first instinctual response was that I needed to say something about this blatant discrimination. When I recalled how the person had directed me into this line because I opened my mouth and said what I needed, I took a deep breath and instead determined to keep my mouth shut. I justified that by saying to myself: All I want to do is to get through this and catch my flight and get to where I need to go. I don't need to get myself into more trouble. I finally got to the front of the line. I went through the ritual of putting my wallet, my belt, my shoes, my keys, my change, my jacket and my bags on the belt of the screening machine. I told myself to keep my mouth shut, and made sure I did not show any emotion.

I went through the screening machine without setting it off. I was also spared having to undergo the body search. Okay, saying nothing and showing nothing seemed to work to help me survive this experience. As I was putting my things back into my pockets, I saw that the young boy was still detained. I grabbed my luggage and headed out toward the gate. A final security person insisted on seeing my ID and ticket again. She was a person of color. Again, I was tempted to say something. Surely she must see what I see. As she was looking at the ticket, my ID, and me, I decided to say nothing. Instead I forced a smile and said, "Thank you." I made my flight with about one minute to spare at the expense of my integrity, dignity, and self-esteem. The guilt, shame, and sense of powerlessness stayed with me all through the rest of my trip.

Many experienced the appeal to be patient for the sake of security as the condition to become fear-bearers—step in line, and do not complain, and you will be okay. Step out of line, and you will be punished. Time and again, I heard people being interviewed on television saying, "If this can keep us safe, I am willing to give up some of my liberties."

On the fifth anniversary of September 11, 2001, our soldiers were fighting a war in Iraq that did not seem to have an end in sight. We were shown daily death and destruction. Periodic reports on television told us that our airports were no safer than before the attacks. Our water supply was still vulnerable. Our borders were not secure. Our ports might be controlled by other countries that had terrorist connections. Yet, we were told again and again to go on with life as usual. Support the economy. Be patient with the inconveniences—all for the sake of security. Follow the rules and don't complain, or you'll be perceived as anti-American—or worse, you might be suspected of being a terrorist. We have been indoctrinated into becoming fear-bearers, and the best we can hope for is to survive. As fear-bearers, we give up many things—our rights, our liberty, our integrity, our dignity—in order to survive. Like Jessica Lynch, survival is supposedly enough to make us into heroes.

Fear-Miners

Fear-conquerors and fear-bearers are often presented to us as the only two options in dealing with our fear. If I cannot fight like Rambo to conquer my fear, the only other option is for me to be a fear-bearer, stepping in line in support of the fear-conquerors just to survive. While I agree that the United States should not become fear-bearers by submitting to the control of the terrorists, I have trouble with the fear-conquerors' course that the nation has taken to conquer its fear. Yet if these were the only two options, being fear-conquerors was the only choice. By becoming fear-conquerors, the United States basically was insisting that the terrorists be the fear-bearers and step in line to our demands. When both sides insisted that the other be fear-bearers, violence was sure to escalate. When the wars began going badly and the people in the United States began to question the fear-conquerors' approach, the fear-conquerors turned inward on their people—forcing those who questioned the validity and legality of the wars into fear-bearers. This is the problem with having only two options in dealing with fear.

Jesus was not a fear-bearer. He did not stay within the safety boundaries set by the religious and political institutions of his time. In fact, he broke many rules for the sake of recognizing the humanity of the poor and powerless people. He refused to practice rituals that were harmful to himself and others. He refused to be a fear-bearer, and crossed the line again and again. As predicted, even by Jesus himself, violence would visit upon him.

Jesus was not a fear-conqueror either. Jesus refused to buy into the assumptions that the Messiah was supposed to be like a rebel or revolutionary, using violence and aggression to liberate the oppressed. When he predicted his suffering and death, his followers—Peter being the most vocal one—were surprised and reacted with disbelief. How could their Messiah be killed? At the time of his arrest, his followers were about to react as fear-conquerors, using aggression and inciting violence. But Jesus stopped them. Jesus taught them that the fear-conqueror's approach to fear was not the way to deal with our fear.

Jesus offered a third alternative. I call people who follow Christ's way of addressing fear "fear-miners." Time and again as recorded in Holy Scriptures, Jesus taught fearful people around him to mine from their fears the wisdom and knowledge of grace, forgiveness, justice, and the seeds of ministry.

> The scribes and the Pharisees brought a woman who had been caught in adultery; and making her stand before all of them, they said to [Jesus], "Teacher, this woman was caught in the very act of committing adultery. Now in the law Moses commanded us to stone such women. Now what do you say?" (Jn. 8:3–5)

This was a fear-filled situation—and not only for the woman, who was facing death. Judging from the reaction of the people around Jesus, their proposed action to follow the law's prescription to punish this woman stemmed from their fear as well. The difference was that the woman was cast as the fear-bearer, and therefore she was to be punished when she crossed the line and broke the rules. The people watching this situation—I presume most of them were men—were cast in the roles of the fear-conquerors. They would conquer their fear by using aggression, which was justified by the law. But the law was not applied equally to everyone. Where was the man who committed adultery with this woman? Maybe he was hiding. Maybe he was one of the men standing around watching. He was not subjected to the same rules because he had more power and would never be cast as a fear-bearer.

When they kept on questioning him, he straightened up and said to them, "Let anyone among you who is without sin be the first to throw a stone at her." And once again he bent down and wrote on the ground. (Jn. 8:7–8)

Jesus exposed the hypocrisy of the situation. He forced the fear-conquerors to look inward at their own fear that caused them to act with aggression toward this woman. Their fear came from their knowledge of the law. If they had broken the laws themselves and if the laws were applied equally to everyone, they could be rejected and publicly humiliated, and would themselves face the possibility of being killed. His question invited them to ponder their fear, linking it to its terrible destination, which would be what the woman was facing. The only difference between them and this woman was that she got caught. When they arrived at that end point, they were able to put their fear in the wider context. They dug below their fear and found the gifts of compassion and mercy, and perhaps a sense of justice.

When they heard it, they went away, one by one, beginning with the elders; and Jesus was left alone with the woman standing before him. Jesus straightened up and said to her, "Woman, where are they? Has no one condemned you?" She said, "No one, sir." And Jesus said, "Neither do I condemn you. Go your way, and from now on, do not sin again." (Jn. 8:9–11)

Jesus then worked with the woman, the fear-bearer. Now that she had almost physically arrived at the terrible most-feared destination—death—she actually encountered Christ. She was not condemned by others, nor was she condemned by Jesus. She had moved from potential death to resurrection in the presence of Christ. In this dangerous exploration, she learned that her fear of condemnation, rejection, and the threat of death should not be the only driving force for her to not break the law. Jesus helped her unearth a primary yearning of God—that she should not sin— because of the grace and love and forgiveness she received from the people in the community, and from God. From this fear-filled situation, Jesus, the fear-miner, invited the fearful parties to dig inward and extract the gems of love, mercy, forgiveness, and justice and thus the essence of living in the community of God.

Jesus, rejecting both the fear-bearer and fear-conqueror approach to fear, took us on a journey to face our fear through his betrayal, suffering, death, and most importantly, resurrection. In his facing the ultimate fear, he exposed the injustice of the world that he lived in. He exposed the unjust application of rules and rituals that oppressed and divided people rather than bringing the community together. As he arrived at that most horrible destination of his journey, he showed us grace and forgiveness, even to those who hurt him. He showed us the greater story of life, which was not about conquering our fear with aggression, nor simply surviving out of our fear of punishment. The greater story of life is not about being afraid of fear, but facing it head on. We are to approach fear as an opening, and as an invitation to mine from it the gifts and treasures buried deep below the surface. When we dig down through fear's openings, we can mine from fear the God-given gifts of wisdom, courage, dignity, and self-esteem with which we can face any adversity that comes our way. When we see our fear as a gift, we will discover that underneath our fear lies the knowledge of God. Buried below our fear is the seed of ministry. Beyond our fear is the hope of resurrection, with new visions for us, our communities, and our nations.

Questions and Activities

1. Select a fear-evoking issue today. Describe it.
2. Fear-Conqueror
   a. In what ways might you be cast in the role of a fear-conqueror?
   b. What will you do when you find yourself being pushed into the fear-conqueror role?
3. Fear-Bearer
   a. In what ways might you be cast in the role of a fear-bearer?
   b. What will you do when you find yourself being cast in the fear-bearer role?
4. Fear-Miner
   a. What would you do to make yourself a fear-miner on this issue?
   b. What gifts and directions for ministries might you discover as a fear-miner?

5

Fear-Exploiter, Fear of God, and Intimacy with God

Now a new king arose over Egypt, who did not know Joseph. He said to his people, "Look, the Israelite people are more numerous and more powerful than we. Come, let us deal shrewdly with them, or they will increase and, in the event of war, join our enemies and fight against us and escape from the land." Therefore they set taskmasters over them to oppress them with forced labor. They built supply cities, Pithom and Rameses, for Pharaoh. But the more they were oppressed, the more they multiplied and spread, so that the Egyptians came to dread the Israelites...And made their lives bitter with hard service in mortar and brick and in every kind of field labor. They were ruthless in all the tasks that they imposed on them. (Ex. 1:8–12, 13–14)

The story of how God delivered the people of Israel from the Egyptians began with "a new king" who "did not know Joseph"— the Joseph who could interpret dreams, the Joseph who contributed a great deal to Egypt with his gifts and abilities and had brought the sons and daughters of Israel to reside in Egypt. The Pharaoh, who did not value history, told his people, the Egyptians, that they should fear the numerous Israelites. Given the right teaching and nurturing, the Egyptians could have responded to their fear by building relationships with the Israelites and creating a community of mutual respect and protection. They could have been fear-miners—discovering, together with the Israelites, new ways to live together—and, in so doing, how to share their resources with each other. But that would have meant Pharaoh might lose his power to control the people. Instead, Pharaoh exploited their fear and encouraged them to act out in aggression—to become fear-conquerors. He evoked fear by telling them that the Israelites could be potential aggressors—they might "join our enemies and fight against us." The Egyptians responded well to this projection of fear, linking the Israelites to the threat of violent attack. This might be one of the oldest records of the doctrine of the preemptive strike. Soon, "the Egyptians came to dread the Israelites." This was the reason why they enslaved the Israelites and "made their lives bitter with hard service." The use of force and aggression was so effective that the Israelites, even though there were more of them, endured the oppression. Most likely, they were fearful of more pain and even death that the Egyptians might inflict on them. The Israelites were forced to be fear-bearers.

Meanwhile, Pharaoh gained two supply cities, Pithom and Rameses, built by the hard labor of the Israelites. Pharaoh was the puppeteer behind the rules and rituals of the oppressors and the oppressed, the fear-conquerors and the fear-bearers. He was the one who exploited the fear of the people to control them, reinforcing his own power. He was the one who ultimately gained from setting up this oppressive condition. Behind the destructive scenario played out by the fear-conquerors and the fear-bearers was the fear-exploiter, who used fear to control others to maintain and increase his power. This was why God, through Moses, intervened. God not only wanted to liberate the Israelites from oppression; he wanted to deal with Pharaoh, the fear-exploiter—the controlling force behind this repeated oppressive human pattern.

Having liberated the Israelites from the grip of Pharaoh, God led the people across the Red Sea into the wilderness. As a free people, they faced an uncertain future. How were they going to organize themselves? Who would tell them what to do? Who would provide safety for them? They complained bitterly to Moses about why he brought them out into the wilderness to die (Ex. 16:3, 17:3). They would rather go back to Egypt, where they lived with clearly defined rules and rituals, oppressive as that had been. All their lives had been "held in slavery by the fear of death." (Heb. 2:15). They knew no other way to live, except to be fear-bearers. They had no role models for relating to each other, except that of the relationship between masters and slaves. Even though they were liberated, they still did not know what it meant to live as a free people. As they organized themselves in this new society, some would inevitably gain more property and power than others. The danger was that they would emulate their former oppressors and become fear-conquerors—and worse, fear-exploiters—using fear to control others to maintain their wealth.

Fear of God

Subsequently, at Mount Sinai, God decided to do something about this potentially destructive response to fear. After God had spoken what we now call the Ten Commandments, in an experience which was like "thunder and lightning, the sound of the trumpet, and the mountain smoking,"

> they were afraid and trembled and stood at a distance, and said to Moses, "You speak to us, and we will listen; but do not let God speak to us, or we will die." Moses said to the people, "Do not be afraid; for God has come only to test you and to put the fear of him upon you so that you do not sin." (Ex. 20:18–20)

God put fear upon the Israelites, through the covenant, to help them not to sin—not to be fear-conquerors in facing their uncertainties in the wilderness. God did that by replacing the fear of other human beings with the fear of God. The fear of God humbled the people into recognizing that they were not gods and that they were not to behave like the Egyptians who had played god and lorded over them all their lives: "I am the Lord your God, who brought you out of the land of Egypt, out of the house of slavery; you shall have no other gods before me" (Ex. 20:2–3).God insisted that the people of Israel treat each other as equals, because there was only one Lord, and that Lord was not to be any human being or any idol fashioned by human hands. The fear of God helped the people of Israel not to sin against each other in the face of uncertainty, doubt, and fear. According to God's covenant with them, they should honor their parents, not murder, not commit adultery, not steal, not bear false witness against their neighbor, and not covet their neighbor's properties. The fear of God stopped them from becoming the puppets of the fear-exploiter while also not becoming fear-conquerors nor fear-bearers. However, would not the fear of God, with all the prescribed rules and rituals be equally oppressive, just like the rules and rituals forced upon the Israelites by Pharaoh and the Egyptians?

> He sent redemption to his people;
>   he has commanded his covenant forever.
> Holy and awesome is his name.
> The fear of the Lord is the beginning of wisdom;
>   all those who practice it have a good understanding.
> His praise endures forever.
>   (Ps. 111: 9–10)

The quality of the fear of God is quite different from the fear and threats evoked by fear-exploiters like Pharaoh. Wole Soyinka, the Nobel Prize recipient in Literature in 1986, gave us an inkling of this distinction when he talked about how human beings responded to the fear prompted by natural disasters as distinct from the fear induced by human beings on each other. The following was what he observed of his neighbors as they dealt with their fear of losing their homes and their livelihood to the fires in southern California during the summer of 2004.

> They were anxious, of course, and fearful. Watchful and insecure. But their humanity was not abused or de-graded by the menace that bore down on them. On the contrary, they remained in combative form, constantly exchanging news as well as tactical suggestions for saving the neighborhood...There exists a vast abyss of sensibilities between the raw force that is Nature, on the one hand, and the exertion of force by one human being in relation to another. I suggest that this has to do with yet another human possession, an attribute that is as much a social acquisition as it is inherent in the human species—dignity.[1]

Perhaps the "fear of God" as described in the Scriptures is more akin to the fear evoked by the forces of nature that Soyinka described. This fear becomes a test of the human spirit to survive, not in a selfish kind of way, but in community, working together and supporting each other. This kind of fear uncovers the strength of human community. In a similar way, the fear of God does not deplete human dignity. It actually shapes and forms respectful

---

[1]Wole Soyinka, *Climate of Fear* (New York: Random House, 2005), 9–10.

human communities. The fear of God, in the form of the covenant, invited the people of Israel to enter into community with a sense of common good and respect for others as equals. The covenant fostered a gracious community in which they could face their fear of uncertainties in the wilderness.

> You who fear the LORD, trust in the LORD!
>   He is their help and their shield.
> The LORD has been mindful of us; he will bless us;...
>   he will bless those who fear the LORD,
>   both small and great.
>   (Ps. 115:11—12a, 13)

The fear of God safeguarded the community by providing rules that, if followed, would foster respectful community. When the rules were broken, when people sinned, there was a way to return to a right relationship with the community and with God through the rituals that God prescribed. This was why the fear of God was a blessing, especially for the "small," weak, and powerless in the community.

If the fear of God was supposed to help us build communities that respect each person's dignity, why did Jesus have so much trouble with the religious leaders of his time regarding the rituals and the laws—from eating with sinners and touching the unclean, to healing people on the Sabbath? The religious leaders of Jesus' time emulated their oppressors (and this time, the oppressors were the Romans) by turning the law of the covenant into threats, using fear to gain control and maintain their power. Instead of teaching the fear of God to foster a community of respect, they exploited people's fear of uncertainty and rejection for their personal gain. They replaced the fear of God with the fear of people who used threats to enforce the law, thereby diminishing people's dignity.

Jesus was quoted as saying twice, "I desire mercy, not sacrifice," to the people who complained that he was eating with sinners and tax collectors and that his disciples were breaking the rules of the Sabbath by picking grain in the field (Mt. 9:13; 12:7). Jesus was teaching the people around him that God did not want them to follow hollow rituals out of the fear of the enforcers of the law. "For I desire steadfast love and not sacrifice / the knowledge of God rather than burnt offerings" (Hos. 6:6).

Jesus, referencing the prophet Hosea, wanted them to know that God desired them to know and love God, and that knowledge would move them to love one another, even those considered sinners, unclean, or enemies. The rituals and rules of the covenant were designed to help people build safer and healthier (both physical and spiritual) communities. Jesus was most disturbed when he saw how the religious leaders had moved people away from understanding the heart and purposes of the rules and rituals of the covenant, by turning the law into an instrument of alienation and oppression, thereby destroying community and distancing people from God. Jesus said:

> "'You shall love the Lord your God with all your heart, and with all your soul, and with all your mind.' This is the greatest and first commandment. And a second is like it, 'You shall love your neighbor as yourself.' On these two commandments hang all the law and the prophets." (Mt. 22:37–40)

To live fully into the rules and rituals set forth by the covenant, we need to know and love God—to be intimate with God. We gladly follow the rules and rituals prescribed by God, not because we are fearful of being punished, but because we know and love God. Jesus is trying to recapture the spirit of the covenant by not only replacing the fear of people with the fear of God, but also by going beyond the fear of God to show us love, knowledge, wisdom, and intimacy with God. He moves us away from the danger of making God into just another human ruler and institution that uses fear to control. He invites us to focus on our relationship as sons and daughters of God, just as he was the Son of God. In his person and ministry, Jesus brings us closer and closer to God, letting us know that God will always be with us, loving us unconditionally. Out of the love of God that we know and experience through Christ, we gladly advance God's commandment to foster community and maintain each person's dignity as children of God.

Fear-Exploiters and Idolatry

The real issue that Jesus had with the fear-exploiters was idolatry. Fear-exploiters try to replace God with their own images. They give the illusion that they are powerful by evoking fear. Through fear, they manipulate others to become fear-conquerors using aggression and punishment to instill fear on others. Through fear, they turn others into fear-bearers who will submit to their control. They have replaced God with themselves. They make themselves into idols to be feared. They play god. When we buy into the fear-exploiter's scheme, we become idolatrous ourselves. If we unreflectively respond to the fear these fear-exploiters evoke and become fear-conquerors, we become puppets of the fear-exploiters, who use aggression to escalate the fear, increasing their power and control. If we respond by being fear-bearers and stay within the status quo, we simply reinforce the power of the fear-exploiters. Fear-conquerors and fear-bearers are co-conspirators with the fear-exploiters, part of the system of idolatry that does not honor God.

Who are the fear-exploiters of our time? It is easy to look around the world scene today and point our fingers at the tyrannical rulers, terrorist organizations, and nations that violate human rights and call them the fear-exploiters. It is true that dictators and terrorists have used fear overtly in the form of threats to control others. In their demonstration of cruelty and violence, they are saying: if you do not do what we demand, you and your loved ones will be hurt or killed. For example, terrorist organizations train people to be fear-conquerors in the most extreme way possible—that of the suicide bombers. They condition the suicide bombers to believe that they can conquer their fear of death for a greater good. In this case, by creating terror and fear among the people whom they think have been doing them wrong, they think they can make those people do what they want them to do. In the end terrorist organizations want control. We can easily and without reservation point our finger at them and say that they are the fear-exploiters of our time. But is it always that simple?

In the United States, we have a tendency to separate people and institutions of the world into those who use fear to rule over others and those that want to do good and spread freedom and democracy. The world is divided into the "good guys" and the "bad guys." But this world is not that simple. In the political scene within the United States, we see politicians on opposing sides of any issue pointing fingers at each other, calling each other fear-exploiters. For example, Republicans called Democrats alarmists when dealing with issues relating to the environment. Democrats called Republicans fear-mongers over the justification of the war in Iraq. Whom should we believe? Who are the real fear-exploiters? If the United States is the "good guy" that loves freedom and democracy, why then do the people in the United States of America live in such a climate of fear? Wole Soyinka described this climate of fear, and my experiences have confirmed this depiction:

Certainly we have learned to associate the emotion of fear with the ascertainable measure of a loss in accustomed volition. The sense of freedom that is enjoyed or, more accurately, taken for granted in normal life becomes acutely contracted. Caution and calculation replace a norm of spontaneity or routine. Often normal speech is reduced to a whisper, even within the intimacy of the home. Choices become limited. One is more guarded, less impulsive.[2]

Of course, we can blame this climate of fear on the terrorists who wish us harm. That, to some extent, is true. However, if we observe more carefully, we also see that this climate of fear was created partly by the United States leaders' response to the threat of the terrorists. Instead of helping its people to work through their fear and to arrive at actions that provide real safety, the leaders of the United States turned inward on its own people, evoking fear to gain control. Soon after the United States invaded Iraq, I was having an informal conversation with a group of theological students and faculty. During the conversation, one faculty mentioned that she had received a petition for peace via the Internet, and she had decided to sign it and sent it on to the congressional representative of her hometown. Another faculty member jokingly said, "So the CIA has you on their list of people to watch." Nervous laughter spread through the room. I thought we had the Bill of Rights to protect citizens of this country. Why would that have even come into the conversation? Because we lived in a climate of fear evoked somehow by our own government that diminished our rights and dignity as citizens.

Let me ask the question again: Who are the fear-exploiters of our time? Is it the United States government? Are they the politicians who want to get reelected? Are they the corporations that want to make sure that they make a profit by controlling the supply and demand of products and resources? Surely, those who have power and influence in any nation, institution, or community have a greater danger of becoming fear-exploiters. If they are not fear-miners, but respond to their own fear by using their power and influence to evoke fear upon others to maintain their sense of security, then yes, they have become fear-exploiters. But I think the realm of the fear-exploiters is not limited to the politically and economically powerful. It is too simplistic to divide people and institutions into those who are powerful and those who are

---

[2]Ibid., 7.

powerless, and to assign the fear-exploiting label to the powerful. This does not explain those who are historically powerless justifying their use of threats and violence to "fight back" or to "survive." Fear-exploiters are not just those whom we call the "bad guys." They are not just the powerful in our society and in the world. Fear-exploiters can be any individual, institution, or entity that evokes fear to control others, and to maintain political and/or economic gain. When a husband subjects his wife and children to constant physical and mental abuse to maintain his sense of control, he is a fear-exploiter. When a landlord uses the tenant's fear of ejection to maintain his or her economic gain, the landlord is a fear-exploiter.[3] The moment a teacher evokes fear to gain control of his or her classroom, that teacher is a fear-exploiter. The moment a student threatens the teacher with accusations of abuse, the student is a fear-exploiter. The moment parents use their power to put fear upon their children to get them to do their homework, or behave in a certain way, they become fear-exploiters. The moment a friend uses threats to control a relationship, she or he has become a fear-exploiter. The moment the owner of a factory uses threats to control the workers, the factory owner becomes a fear-exploiter. The moment an activist group uses violence and destructive threats to achieve its well-justified goals, it has become a fear-exploiter. The moment a corporation evokes fear to control the market, to get people to buy its products, it is a fear-exploiter. The moment we use fear to get someone to become a member of our religious group, we are fear-exploiters.

If any individual, community, institution, or nation can become a fear-exploiter, how can we stop ourselves from participating in this form of idolatry? We start by recognizing the way of the fear-exploiters.

Like the Pharaoh who did not know Joseph, fear-exploiters do not want us to remember the truth and learn lessons from our history. Instead, fear-exploiters want to define history, choosing those historical "facts" that reinforce their power.

The fear-exploiters use the fear of rejection, isolation, chaos, psychological and physical harm, and death to maintain control. In effect, the message is: if you don't do what we want, you will be excluded and harm will come to you.

The fear-exploiters redefine the rules to give them advantages and to maintain their power. By defining the rules, the fear-

---
[3]Ibid., 106.

exploiters define reality for others. They want this reality eventually to become accepted as daily rituals to be followed unquestioningly. The fear-exploiters propagate a spirituality of scarcity. They project a reality that says sufficient resources, power, and love are never available. Therefore, be competitive, take and keep, and be suspicious of those who have more. The fear-exploiters will cast this false reality in the name of whatever is the popular concept or language of the time. They will give the impression of peace without justice. They will sell the illusion of intimacy without love. They will promise security and safety while continuing to project fear. They will sell us symbolic substitutes that promise to make us safe while the goal is to keep us craving for more.

The fear-exploiters have an inherent fear of community, because if a community of respect and trust decided to come together and tell the truth about the people's experiences, the fear-exploiters' scheme would be exposed. Therefore, fear-exploiters want to divide communities by spreading misinformation about one group or another within that community. When the different factions in the community are not able to work together, the fear-exploiters stay in control. The fear-exploiters create distrust so that the people become suspicious of others. Where there is no trust, there is no truth telling. When there is no truth telling, there is no intimacy. When there is no intimacy, there is no community.

The fear-exploiters evoke fear to condition some in the community to be fear-conquerors. They become foot soldiers in enforcing the rules and ritual. The fear-exploiters want to turn most people into fear-bearers, supporting the status quo without questions. The fear-exploiters want to diminish our self-esteem and take away our dignity so that we do not trust our own ability to work through our fear. Punishment and conditional love are the weapons that fear-exploiters employ. Do what we want, and you will be loved. Cross the line, and you will be punished.

The fear-exploiters use diversion to distract people from seeing and addressing the real issues. They do not want people to work together for real safety and security. The fear-exploiters pile fear upon fear to overwhelm people so they will buy whatever substitutes promise to alleviate their fear for the moment. The fear-exploiters want to keep people in a constant state of fear—afraid of fear itself. The more the people avoid fear, the stronger the fear-exploiters will be in maintaining and increasing their control and power. "For our struggle is not against enemies of blood and flesh, but against the rulers, against the authorities, against the cosmic powers of this present darkness, against the spiritual forces of evil in the heavenly places" (Eph. 6:12).

A spiritual force consistently wants to replace God with the escalation of fear, which diminishes our dignity, destroys the possibility of intimacy and community, and separates us from God. This fear-exploiter shifts in shape and form. It can reside in an individual. It can take over a community. It can control a nation. Fear-exploiters are the rulers, authorities, powers, angels, heights, depths, and even death itself that Paul talked about when he listed all that strives to separate us from the love of God (Rom. 8:37–39).

Refusing to Be Fear-Exploiters

To stop ourselves from becoming fear-exploiters, we must be a people who remember our history—to honor its gifts and learn from our mistakes. We must take the time to reflect on what kind of power and influence we have, and not use it to evoke fear over others to maintain our power and control. Instead, we must exercise our power and influence to build trust among people, creating a community of respect. We must learn to be fear-miners— discovering the gift of ministry behind our fear. For those who have found themselves forced into the roles of the fear-bearers, we need to develop a community of trust in which we can tell the truth about our experience.[4] In doing so, we discover our God-given dignity that no one, or no institution, can take away.

For those who are cast in the roles of the fear-conquerors, we need to ask ourselves: Who stands to benefit from our use of aggression against others whom we are told are our enemies? We need to see clearly the consequences of our aggressive actions. We need to have the courage to reach across the division set by the fear-exploiters and listen to the fear-bearers' experiences. Fear-conquerors and fear-bearers need to come together and tell the truth, and in the process expose the fear-exploiter's scheme, and together repent of their idolatry.[5]

---

[4]The best work that describes this process is Paulo Freire, *Pedagogy of the Oppressed* (New York: Continuum, 1970).

[5]A great example of this movement was the work of Commission on Truth and Reconciliation in South Africa, in which the community gathered together to listen to the witnesses, the experiences of the victims' families, and the perpetrators of the crime. See Desmond Tutu, *No Future Without Forgiveness* (New York: Doubleday, 2000).

We need to replace our fear of the fear-exploiters and return to the fear of God. The fear of God reminds us that we are not God and we are not to play God by becoming fear-exploiters. We must live the spirituality of abundance, which begins with the unconditional love of God.[6] God never runs out of love and grace for us. We know this through our relationship with Jesus Christ. In that trust, we act according to the purpose of God's pattern of behavior—to create a trusting, respectful community to do justice, love mercy, and walk humbly with God (Mic. 6:8). With this knowledge of God, we take risks to follow in Christ's footsteps, refusing to be fear-conquerors or fear-bearers. In the love of God, we have the courage to follow Christ all the way to the cross, exposing the exploiters' hollow scheme: "Through death [Jesus] might destroy the one who has the power of death, that is, the devil, and free those who all their lives were held in slavery by the fear of death" (Heb. 2:14b–15).

Following Christ, we can disarm the fear-exploiters by facing the most terrible destination of fear that they can inflict on a human being. In moving from death to resurrection, we break out of the control of the fear-exploiter.

> When you were buried with him in baptism, you were also raised with him through faith in the power of God, who raised him from the dead...He disarmed the rulers and authorities and made a public example of them, triumphing over them in it. (Col. 2:12, 15)

Intimacy with God, through Jesus Christ, is our true security. In that trust and knowledge of God, we reaffirm our inherent gifts of dignity and self-esteem. In that knowledge of God, we find our safety in creating intimate relationships with others. In these networks of God-fearing/loving relationships, we create trustful communities that speak the truth and expose the fear-exploiters wherever they attempt to possess us as individuals, communities, institutions, or nations.

> For I am convinced that neither death, nor life, nor angels, nor rulers, nor things present, nor things to come, nor powers, nor height, nor depth, nor anything else in all creation, will be able to able to separate us from the love of God in Christ Jesus our Lord. (Rom. 8:37–39)

---

[6]I explored the spirituality of abundance in Eric H. F. Law, *Inclusion* (St. Louis: Chalice Press, 2000), 29–37.

Questions and Activities

1. How do you recognize the way of the fear-exploiter?
2. Consider the descriptors of the fear-exploiters in this chapter. They:
   a. Do not want us know the truth.
   b. Do not want us to learn from history. In some cases, they distort history to make themselves look good.
   c. Use threats, bullying, rejection, isolation, and chaos to maintain their control.
   d. Impose new rules that favor themselves over others.
   e. Propagate the spirituality of scarcity.
   f. Create chaos and divisions.
   g. Destroy community.
   h. Use fear to make fear-conquerors, who then force others to be fear-bearers.
3. As you consider the list of traits of the fear-exploiters, what individuals and groups come to mind as fitting these descriptions within your community, state and nation, particularly within the last year?
4. What power or influence do you have to expose the fear-exploiters? What influence do you have to bring the community together to stop playing the roles of fear-conquerors and fear-bearers?
5. In what ways can you replace the fear of the fear-exploiters with the fear of God?
6. Name a natural disaster you were part of, or have heard/read about. What were the constructive things that people in the community did or shared during and after the disaster? How might these observations help you understand the phrase: "The fear of God is the beginning of wisdom?"

6

Finding Intimacy in a
World of Fear

The summer of 1974 was the first major turning point in my life. I was seventeen years old and had been accepted by Cornell University. Along with the orientation package that arrived in the mail, I found an invitation to a special orientation for "minority students" sponsored by an organization called COSEP (Committee on Special Educational Projects). This meant that I would be arriving on the Cornell campus two weeks before the rest of students. As an Asian student and someone who had spent all my life in an urban environment, going to Cornell was exciting, but also quite fearful. I knew I would be entering a predominately European American environment. Being seventeen, I would also be slightly younger than most of the students. I also had a fear of not being able to meet the academic challenge at Cornell. I had only been living in the United States for three and a half years. My English skills were my weakness, and this showed in my SAT score. My fears caused me to pay attention to this invitation, and I gladly accepted it.

The day I arrived on campus, other students of color greeted me warmly. At our first meeting that evening, I noticed about fifty students of racially and economically diverse backgrounds. We would live, work, and play together in the almost-empty campus for the next two weeks. The leaders, most of whom were juniors and seniors, took us on tours to explore the different parts of the campus. They familiarized us with the various programs available to help us with our social and academic lives. The program addressed our fear of this unknown environment by helping us gain knowledge of the physical environment and develop relationships, which led to trust among the students and the institution. As we gained more knowledge of the institution, we were not afraid of it, but were able to "work the system" to get what we needed. In this trusting environment, we told the truth about our apprehensions, and our need for support, both personally and academically. We learned to trust in our own ability to succeed in this new place with the help of a community of people who would not shame us if we asked for help. We did not need to be fear-conquerors, nor did we need to be fear-bearers.

A Community of Trust and Our Fears

Building a community of trust is the most effective way to address fears. Trust comes from knowledge. When we do not know our environment, our fear level rises. When our knowledge of the environment increases, we have less fear. The best way to enter an unknown environment and not be paralyzed by fear is to do it in a community in which we have intimate relationships with others— friends, coworkers, loved ones, and family. In that trust, we can take the risk to share our fears, face them, and work through them together. The reason why my experience at the COSEP orientation was so important was that through the intimate relationships developed in that trustful community, we could rely on each other to explore the new terrain. Our situation could be compared to a platoon of soldiers entering into a dangerous unknown environment. They have to rely on their close relationships and knowledge of each other's skills and abilities to accomplish their goals. They gain this knowledge and trust of each other through their training and living together. Firefighters and police officers, who often are sent into unknown and dangerous environments, must have relationships of trust based on knowledge of each person in the group.

Trust comes from knowledge and relationships—both with self and with others. I trust my own ability because I know my own strengths and weaknesses. The more I know myself, the more secure I am when I encounter others who are different. Therefore, I am not afraid to venture into unknown situations or to reach out to encounter another person or to take on a new task. My trust of myself comes from my knowledge of myself.

I trust the associates with whom I have worked for many years because we know each other well enough to speak the truth to each other. We may have conflicts and disagreements at times, but we know our relationship will still be there to sustain us. In the act of making love, I know my partner so well that I can show my physical self, being totally vulnerable because I know our respect for each other as whole persons will always be there. Trust achieved through knowledge and relationship, which is intimacy, is the best remedy for dealing with our fear—there is no substitute.

Yet, plenty of substitutes offer themselves out there. Marketers have again figured out that a world full of projection of fears also teems with the yearning for intimacy. A soft drink commercial I saw on television proved this. We see a young man leaving the movie theater with his date. He is insecure and afraid, perhaps fearful of rejection. He says goodbye to his date. He walks away, regretting his decision to say goodbye so soon. Then he drinks a few sips of this soft drink and suddenly becomes brave. He runs back toward his date, who is getting into a taxi. He grabs her courageously and kisses her. Intimacy is achieved; fear is conquered. All you need to do is to buy and drink this product.

This commercial tells us that a large number of people are yearning for intimacy but do not know how to achieve it. This commercial doesn't tell us how to get on the path to real intimacy, such as building trust through developing a relationship. This commercial wants us to buy a symbolic substitute that can instantly turn us from being a fear-bearer to a fear-conqueror.

I was in a strange town in a hotel room that looked like every other hotel room. I had been teaching for five days and I was tired. I missed the familiarity of my home, my friends, and my loved ones. I mindlessly turned on the television and clicked my clicker to change channels. I came upon a music video. The singer, whom I did not recognize, was looking straight at me. In the extreme close-up shot, I could see this singer's eyelashes, sparkling eyes, and moist lips. I could see her tongue licking her teeth. She did not sing her song—she whispered it. She was whispering directly to me, it seemed. In real life to hear someone whisper, I have to be very close to that person—close enough, in fact, to see that person's eyelashes. As this video drew me in, I realized that this was just an illusion of intimacy. How many people had I gotten close enough to that I could see their eyelashes in real life? What was this illusion of intimacy doing to me and to all those who were watching the same images? In a world of communicable diseases and interpersonal violence, relationships were considered a risk and a liability. In this illusion of intimacy, no risk was involved.

This video supplied me with a symbolic substitute of intimacy with no real contact, without trust, without relationship, without love.

The world of electronic media knows they can make great profit by providing substitutes for intimacy. Go to a rock concert, and you will experience a kind of fake intimacy. A rock singer can whisper into a microphone. Thousands of people listen in the audience— each of whom gets the illusion the performer is whispering closely and directly to him or her. Pornography is a prime example of this false intimacy. A person watching moving images of people having sex with close-up shots at very inconceivable angles is only getting a temporary fix of this need for intimacy. In real life, to get that close to someone—whether in a sexual act or not—requires the building of trust founded on knowledge and relations—for example, trust between a doctor and a patient, or trust between two lovers.

Lying in my bed alone in that nondescript hotel room, I realized I needed to go home and be with my family, my loved ones, and my friends soon. I needed to be close to someone I trust, someone with whom I have developed an intimate relationship. I needed to hold hands, get a hug that lingered long enough for me to feel accepted, and share a meal with friends, engaging each other in insightful and revealing dialogue.

I got on a plane to go home the next day. That particular Friday the flight was completely full. After the flight took off and I settled into my seat, I noticed that the plane was very quiet. Three hundred and fifty people, and nobody was talking to anybody. On the one hand, I understood. Like me, all these people probably had worked all week. They were tired and did not want to talk at all. On the other hand, something was unnatural about 350 people cramped into this small space, practically touching elbows, yet nobody acknowledging or talking to each other.

In the middle of the cabin sat a young child next to her young mother. She was about two. Without warning, she said in a loud screech, "I'm afraid of the plane!" I watched the reaction of the other passengers. There was none—not an outward sign from anyone acknowledging this child's fear. Her mother, however, was totally embarrassed by her child's breaking the unspoken etiquette in this plane.

"Shush…" She gave the little girl a stern look as she said, "I don't think the gentlemen next to you want to hear what you have to say."

When this initial effort to keep her quiet did not work, the mother started threatening her. She actually said, "Do you want me to punch you in the face? Do you?"

The poor little girl said, "No."

"Why not?" her mother asked.

The little girl was silent. All this time the man sitting next to the little girl never said a word or attempted to connect with her. The whole plane heard this, but nobody reacted. The sad part was that I was doing the same thing. I thought people had a real yearning for intimacy. Here was a chance to make connection with a child who was willing to be vulnerable and tell the truth. But nobody took a risk and returned this offering to be intimate. Instead, she was silenced into being a fear-bearer like all of us on the plane, with her mother serving as the fear-conqueror. We had a need and yearning for intimacy. And yet we did not know how to achieve it.

Foot Washing, Intimacy, and Fear

For the rest of the flight I was preparing a sermon for Maundy Thursday of Holy Week. At this church at which I was to preach, their tradition had been to do a foot-washing ritual. I was specifically asked by the leaders of the church to preach a sermon that would encourage people to participate in this ritual during the service. As I read about Jesus washing his disciples' feet before he was betrayed, I tried to imagine the people in this plane washing each other's feet. If these people were in church on Maundy Thursday, what would I say to them to get them to consider washing each other's feet?

> [Jesus] got up from the table, took off his outer robe, and tied a towel around himself. Then he poured water into a basin and began to wash the disciples' feet and to wipe them with the towel that was tied around him. He came to Simon Peter, who said to him, "Lord, are you going to wash my feet?" Jesus answered, "You do not know now what I am doing, but later you will understand." Peter said to him, "You will never wash my feet." Jesus answered, "Unless I wash you, you have no share with me." (Jn. 13:4–8)

Washing someone's feet is a very intimate thing. I can imagine Jesus looking at each of the disciples, speaking to each one softly, touching their feet, washing and drying them. Jesus knew that his followers would be facing many fears in the days to come when he would be betrayed and condemned to suffer and die. By washing their feet, he was demonstrating to them that intimacy with him and each other was the best preparation for facing and working through their fears. Peter, who often expressed what we are thinking, resisted this gesture of intimacy. He said, "You will never wash my feet." Why? Because Peter, like many of us, had set ideas of what was proper. He might have been thinking, "You are Jesus, my teacher; you are not supposed to serve me. You are supposed to be served and waited upon."

Role Prescribing, Fears, and Service

We put distance between others and ourselves by prescribing roles to one another. You can fill in the blanks for the following sentences:

You are a teacher, you are not supposed to _____.

You are a priest, you are not supposed to _____.

You are a Christian, you are not supposed to _____.

You are a mother or a father, you are not supposed to _____.

You are a husband or a wife, you are not supposed to _____.

You are gay, you are not supposed to _____.

You are straight, you are not supposed to _____.

You are Asian, you are not supposed to _____.

You are disabled, you are not supposed to _____.

You are a man, a woman, a son, a daughter, a mother-in-law, a father-in-law; you are not supposed to _____.

Jesus, by his action, was teaching his disciples that to be intimate with one another, with him, and with God, they had to put aside these prescribed roles that put distance between them. When we are able to put aside the presumptions we have about each other, we have made the first step toward intimacy.

Jesus was also teaching them that to be intimate with the other, they had to serve the other. Independent of the role one plays in a relationship, one must put the roles aside and serve others. This is especially important for the powerful and influential people in the community. When we serve others, we have taken the second step toward intimacy.

Jesus was teaching them that to be intimate with others, they had to allow others to serve them. It takes two to be intimate. If we refuse to be served, like Peter, because of what we think should or should not happen, we are rejecting that intimacy. When we allow ourselves to be served, we have taken the third step toward achieving intimacy. Intimacy involves a reciprocal exchange of power. To serve and to be served and then to serve again; to receive and to give and to receive again; these are the actions that move a relationship toward a fuller and deeper intimacy.

Finally, Jesus taught his followers that this intimacy was to be shared with more and more people. Intimacy is the only way we can break the invisible walls that separate us. Sharing this intimacy, exchanging gift and power is the only way to create a Christlike community of trust through which we can address our fear. In this intimate trustful community, we come alive in realizing the realm of God.

Are you willing to be close to another person by allowing yourselves to be served and to serve others?

Are you willing to be close to Christ by allowing Christ to serve you and then learn to serve others by imitating Christ?

Are you willing to be close to God by allowing God to serve you, to love you, even though you might think that you do not deserve it?

Fears and Choices

Once, when [Jesus] was in one of the cities, there was a man covered with leprosy. When he saw Jesus, he bowed with his face to the ground and begged him, "Lord, if you choose, you can make me clean." The Jesus stretched out his hand, touched him, and said, "I do choose. Be made clean." Immediately the leprosy left him. And he ordered him to tell no one. "Go," he said, "and show yourself to the priest, and, as Moses commanded, make an offering for your cleansing, for a testimony to them." (Lk. 5:12–14)

A leper was considered unclean and excluded from the religious and social life of Jesus' time. Whoever touched the leper would also be considered unclean (Num. 19:22). Most people would not touch anyone who was considered unclean because of their fear of rejection.

Jesus was confronted with a choice. Jesus knew that fear-exploiters were using the rules and rituals surrounding who was clean and who was unclean to divide the community that the rules and rituals were prescribed to support. He fought against this exploitation of the law by choosing consciously to break the rules and reach across the fear barriers to achieve intimacy that he knew God so desired. So Jesus chose to touch the leper and make him clean.

Later in the gospel of Luke, Jesus was confronted with a lawyer's question of "Who is my neighbor?" Jesus replied:

> "A man was going down from Jerusalem to Jericho, and fell into the hands of robbers, who stripped him, beat him, and went away, leaving him half dead. Now by chance a priest was going down that road; and when he saw him, he passed by on the other side. So likewise a Levite, when he came to the place and saw him, passed by on the other side. But a Samaritan while traveling came near him; and when he saw him, he was moved with pity. He went to him and bandaged his wounds, having poured oil and wine on them. Then he put him on his own animal, brought him to an inn, and took care of him. The next day he took out two denarii, gave them to the innkeeper, and said, Take care of him; and when I come back, I will repay you whatever more you spend.' Which of these three, do you think, was a neighbor to the man who fell into the hands of the robbers?" [The lawyer] said, "The one who showed him mercy." Jesus said to him, "Go and do likewise." (Lk. 10:30–37)

If the priest or the Levite decided to help this person and on the way to get help the person died, the law required he go through an elaborate ritual cleansing before he could touch food or any other person: "Any who are unclean but do not purify themselves, those persons shall be cut off from the assembly, for they have defiled the sanctuary of the LORD." (Num. 19:20).

I can see why such a rule was necessary to lower the risk of spreading diseases, protecting the health of the people in the community. And the ritual cleansing provided a way for people to reenter the community. These rules and rituals were supposed to uphold the well-being of the community. Unfortunately, such rules were often used to exclude many, especially the powerless.

The rules could be used to evoke fear in those whom they wanted to control. Once a person was declared unclean, he or she was shunted into a category of a different kind, no longer considered a human being. People did not need to treat them as equals anymore. A distance was created between the clean and the unclean. The "unclean" could be ignored. The "clean" could dismiss their own sense of right and wrong, and even their compassion, because the "unclean" were not like them.

Jesus told this lawyer that a person could choose to be a good neighbor to another, like the Samaritan, who chose to touch this "half-dead" person. If we put ourselves in the position of the Jew who fell into the hands of robbers, we see that Jesus was again telling us that allowing ourselves to be served, even by a historical enemy such as a Samaritan, was part of God's yearning for us. Jesus chose to touch the unclean. Jesus chose to eat with the tax collectors. Jesus chose to talk to a Samaritan woman at the well. Jesus chose to be close to those who were considered outsiders and outcasts. Jesus chose to encounter those whom others considered sinners or enemies. In doing so, Jesus chose intimacy to counter the exclusive response to fear.

In the end, Jesus calls us to choose. We can choose to reach around the fear-enforced rules and rituals that separate us and make connection with others. We can choose not to buy symbolic substitutes that only give us the illusion of safety and intimacy. We can choose not to be fear-bearers. We can choose not to be fear-conquerors. We can choose not to be fear-exploiters. We can choose to break the rules to tell the truth, exposing the fear-exploiters in our midst. We can choose to be fear-miners, enabling others and ourselves to discover the gifts of ministry. We can choose to develop a community of trusting relationships through which we can work together on the things that will provide us with true security—such as keeping the environment clean and healthy for future generations, making sure people have adequate healthcare, ensuring people's livelihood when they cannot work, creating community and civic organizations that truly protect everyone's dignity, rights, and safety. We can choose to be intimate with ourselves. We can choose to be intimate with others who are different. We can choose to be intimate with our enemies. We can choose to touch and be touched, give and receive, serve and be served, cleanse and be cleansed. We can choose to be intimate with Christ. We can choose to be intimate with God.

"Come," my heart says, "seek his face!"
Your face, Lord, do I seek.
Do not hide your face from me.
(Ps. 27:8)

Questions and Activities

1. Recall an experience in which you knew you were able to deal with your fear constructively.
   a. Who was there?
   b. What was said and done?
   c. How did you know you were safe?
2. What are the elements of a community of trust that truly address our fears?
3. How can you make truth be part of a trusting community?
4. How are relationships crucial to building a community of trust?
5. What do truth and relationship have to do with intimacy? With self? With others? With creation? With God?
6. Name the substitutes for true intimacy you see today. What real intimacy do the substitutes seek to replace? How can you avoid or reject the substitute and go for the real thing?
7. If you have participated in a foot-washing ritual, describe it. What fear did it trigger in you before the ritual? How did you overcome that fear? What did you learn about intimacy from this experience?
8. What are the elements of true security? At home? At work? In school? In church? In the neighborhood? For the earth?
9. Every time a fear is triggered within you, you can make choices to actively move away from the destructive, alienating reactions and move toward the constructive, fear-mining actions. Name a fear and work through the following list of actions. For each action, write down how you would go about doing it.
   1. Name and break away from rules that divide and alienate.
   2. Find, share, and uphold rules that connect and build community.
   3. Name the rituals that do not really help.
   4. Find and enact the rituals (liturgies) that truly address your fear.
   5. Name and avoid technologies that divide and isolate.
   6. Learn to use technologies in ways that connect you with others forming communities of action and resistance.

7. Avoid buying symbolic substitutes for safety.
8. Gather in community to explore what true safety is and how to cultivate it.
9. Avoid buying symbolic substitutes for intimacy.
10. Gather in community to engage people in building trusting relationships through which truth can be shared.
11. Resist being a fear-bearer.
12. Refuse to be a fear-conqueror.
13. Abstain from being a fear-exploiter, tempting as it may be.
14. Be a truth teller and find ways to name and expose the fear-exploiters.
15. Learn to be a fear-miner.
16. Achieve intimacy with self.
17. Foster intimacy with others who are different.
18. Advance intimacy with your enemies.
19. Grow in intimacy with Christ.
20. Find intimacy with God.

7

What Are You Doing Here?

*Then the word of the LORD came to him, saying,
"What are you doing here, Elijah?" He answered, "I have
been very zealous for the LORD, the God of hosts; for the
Israelites have forsaken your covenant, thrown down your
altars, and killed your prophets with the sword. I alone
am left, and they are seeking my life, to take it away."*
*[The LORD] said, "Go out and stand on the mountain
before the LORD, for the LORD is about to pass by." Now
there was a great wind, so strong that it was splitting
mountains and breaking rocks in pieces before the LORD,
but the LORD was not in the wind; and after the wind
an earthquake, but the LORD was not in the earthquake;
and after the earthquake a fire, but the LORD was not in
the fire; and after the fire a sound of sheer silence. When
Elijah heard it, he wrapped his face in his mantle and
went out and stood at the entrance of the cave. Then there
came a voice to him that said, "What are you doing here,
Elijah?" He answered, "I have been very zealous for the
LORD, the God of hosts; for the Israelites have forsaken
your covenant, thrown down your altars, and killed your
prophets with the sword. I alone am left, and they are
seeking my life, to take it away." Then the LORD said to
him, "Go, return on your way to the wilderness of Damas-
cus; when you arrive, you shall anoint Hazael as king over
Aram. Also, you shall anoint Jehu son of Nimshi as king
over Israel; and you shall anoint Elisha son of Shaphat of
Abel-meholah as prophet in your place.*
(1 Kings 19:9b–16)

Fearful for his life because of Queen Jezebel, Elijah escaped into the wilderness. After journeying in the wilderness for forty days, he came upon a cave on Mount Horeb, the mountain of God. The first thing God said to him was, "What are you doing here?"

Elijah answered with his usual complaint—I have been good, but they are after me, and I'm all alone. Then God instructed him to go outside and stand on the mountain to meet God. But wasn't God already talking to him? Why then did God ask Elijah to go and meet him? Elijah might have been talking to God, but he had not met and known God. He had no intimate relationship with God. In this fearful time, God longed for Elijah to know God and to know what God was not. Elijah wanted God to come to him as the thunder, the wind, the earthquake, and the fire—all the things in nature that evoke fear in us. But God was not there. God was in the silence. In the traditional King James translation, God was in the "still small voice." Contrast the presence of God in this story to the presence of God on Mount Sinai. God did not present herself in the traditional fear-evoking images. God's way of working through our fear is not through violence and aggression that evokes more fear in others, but through listening to the sheer silence—that is the voice of the Holy. In this untraditional image of God—silence—a voice asked Elijah again, "What are you doing here?"

Elijah still did not understand what God was trying to tell him because he reiterated his old complaint—I have been good, and they are after me; I'm all alone. God then instructed him to go back and anoint people—the king of Aram, the king of Israel, and his own successor. One principle role/ministry of the prophet was to anoint. By asking Elijah, "What are you doing here?" God was trying to tell Elijah to focus on what he was called to do. In doing so, he would have allies who would support his ministry; and he would have a disciple who would follow him and carry on his ministry with him and after him. Elijah would not be alone anymore. By refocusing Elijah on the purpose of his role in ministry, God moved Elijah from a fearful paralyzed state to a proactive movement of empowerment of himself and others. He could return to face his fear, no longer alone, and function as a part of a network, a community of faithful people.

In 1979, I finally accepted the call to serve as an ordained minister through the Episcopal Church. I could use my established residency with any of three different church communities in three different dioceses to move through the process to becoming a priest—the Chinese mission in Chinatown in the Diocese of New York; a church in Jackson Heights, Queens, where my family lived at that time in the Diocese of Long Island; or the Episcopal Church at Cornell, where I went to college in the Diocese of Central New York. I chose to enter the process through the Diocese of Central New York because I was afraid of being "stuck" in a Chinese ministry. I have seen quite a few burnt-out Chinese priests working exclusively in Chinese ministries with little support from their dioceses.

I thought if I went through New York or Long Island with their large Chinese populations, I would have to deal with the "stereotypical" expectation to serve in a Chinese-language ministry. I was fearful that if my first job was with a Chinese ministry, I would be stuck there with little possibility of movement into other kinds of ministries. Then in ten years, I would become a bitter, overworked, underpaid priest; in twenty years, I would feel a sense of incompetence and find myself living in depression. In thirty years, I would die of stress, high blood pressure, and heart attack. I might have been being a little dramatic, but I had seen Asian clergy who had gone through exactly that scenario.

At the recommendation of a mentor after I finished my first year in theological school, I decided to face my fear head on. At that time in Boston, a new Chinese ministry was developing at the Cathedral. The congregation consisted of mostly Chinese refugees from Vietnam and Cambodia. I entered into a field-education learning contract with the priest in charge, who was a man learned in Chinese and English. He preached with a Chinese vocabulary that was both accessible and theologically sound. His presence in the eucharist was spirit-filled, mainly through his use of the Cantonese language placing effective accent on specific words and phrases. I had a ninth grade level of Chinese language skills. Through high school and college in the United States, I had not used my Chinese language skills at all. At times I felt completely incompetent standing next to this gifted and learned minister. Fortunately, he was an excellent supervisor who was able to push me and nurture me at the same time. It was not easy, but I was learning a lot.

One year later, my supervisor left to start another mission on the West Coast. My worst fear had come true. I was on my own, stuck, alone. At first, I was trying to emulate the priest who had left. Within a month, I realized that as a part-time minister, still trying to finish my theological study, this was impossible. I felt like running away to hide. But I knew running was not an option. What was I afraid of? I was afraid that I would be perceived as incompetent. Then I would get a bad evaluation and recommendation for my final application to become a priest. I would not be ordained. I would lose my self-esteem once more; and, this time, I might not recover, etc. As I linked my fear toward its ultimate destination, I became almost depressed. There seemed to be no way out.

Facing this dead-end street, I prayed. As I prayed, I heard a voice asking me, "Eric, what are you doing here?" I said, "I have been good and faithful in following Your call to ministry. I was courageous to face my fear and decided to work in this ministry. Why have You abandoned me? I am all alone." As I complained, I heard the question again, "What are you doing here, Eric?"

Having said what I needed to say, I calmed down. The question echoed in my head again and again, and I began to answer it. I was not here to imitate another person or show that I was competent in the eyes of others. I was called be a child of God among these wonderful people who gathered around Christ's table, watching me struggle through the sermon and liturgy in Chinese, and still loved and respected me. At that moment, I knew what I was going to do.

I started a monthly gathering at different church members' homes. At these gatherings, we would share food and a time of Bible reflection followed by a time of sharing of concerns and prayers. I was not the one in charge of these events. Each church member took turn in the leadership. Every month, excitement would build as we prepared to gather at another church member's home. They arranged for everyone's transportation, made the food, and packed it to travel. One month we would be eating, singing, and praying in an expensive condo in Cambridge. The next month, we would be laughing and praying in a one-room apartment in a low-income housing project sitting on chairs made out of cardboard boxes and crates. The location was not important as long as we had storytelling, laughter, food, and genuine concern for each individual and family. I remember fondly many moments at these gathering during which I sat back, silently thanking God that I was not alone. A small voice echoed in my head, "This is why I am here." I still struggled with the Chinese liturgy and sermon on Sunday, but the monthly gathering became true communion for this community.

What I learned from the years I served this ministry was that I was not very good at serving a Chinese community in its traditional form and expectations of a priest. Yet, I was called to stay connected with the Asian communities, but in ways that might not be what others expected. By living fully with this fear, I mined from it a new vision for how I could serve, using my talents and gifts. As I was graduating from seminary, I was able to say "no," without shame or guilt, to the part-time Chinese Ministry positions offered to me. Instead, I accepted a call to be the campus minister at the University of Southern California. As soon as I settled in Los Angeles, I immediately applied for a grant to begin a ministry with Asian youth and young adults. The program nurtured Asian young people, helping them face their fear as people living in-between cultures and communities. The overall goal was to enable them to become effective leaders in their own church communities. Eventually, this program became the model for a provincial program offering an annual training program for Asian American youth and young adults in the West Coast dioceses and Hawaii. In another three years, the program became a national program.

Miriam Greenspan wrote:

> Joyful living is not the same thing as living without fear. It's about living fully with fear. Joy is what we find when we act with our fear for the sake of life. Mindful fear moves us to act with courage and loving-kindness, in the service of ourselves and others. And these acts of compassion and service are the quickest route to dispelling fear. If you're afraid of illness, serve someone who's ill. If you're afraid of disability, serve someone who's disabled. If you're afraid of not having enough money, work for the poor. If you're afraid of death, volunteer at a hospice. If you're afraid of loneliness, work with the elderly shut-ins in nursing homes. Then you will discover the alchemy of fear. Facing into our worst fears—of death, loss, pain, vulnerability, isolation and chaos— takes as much courage as trekking in the wilderness in a snow storm...[F]inding the core of our fear, we find our way. [1]

At the beginning of 2006, I started a new ministry called the Kaleidoscope Institute. The goal of the Institute was to train competent leaders in a diverse and changing world. This ministry was a recreation of the Kaleidoscope Project, a training program for

---

[1]Miriam Greenspan, *Healing Through the Dark Emotions* (Boston & London: Shambhala, 2004), 196.

groups of churches offering a combination of skills for congregation development and for building inclusive community. I had successfully implemented this project in three Episcopal dioceses and two United Methodist conferences. The institute would have a new focus of leadership formation and local church community development. As I formulated this new organization, I created a line-up of workshops for local church leaders. I was sure that these programs would be successful. However, as February and March and April rolled by, the registrations for these programs were not coming in as I had expected. My increased effort in sending out more e-mails and notices did not seem to help. With only two or three persons registered, I was reluctant to cancel these programs until the very day before. I was hoping that a miracle would happen, when people would suddenly realize that they needed these programs.

I finally pulled back and asked: What am I afraid of? I decided to take a walk in the wilderness. I was fearful of people perceiving me as a failure. This would lead me to think that I, in fact, was a failure. The lack of interest in these programs might mean that I was no longer relevant in my writing and my consulting work. And this would lead to no income. I would go into financial trouble, and so on and so on. The linkage work led me, of course, to chaos, vulnerability, rejection, and even death.

As I journeyed in the wilderness, I realized how unfounded my fear was: I was not going to die or lose my livelihood if the Kaleidoscope Institute did not succeed as I had envisioned it. I had successfully made an income doing God's work before the Institute; I could still do it with or without the Institute. Having assured myself of that, I cancelled every program in May and June and gave myself an even longer stay in the wilderness.

In the wilderness, I heard the question that God asked me every time I was afraid: What are you doing here, Eric? I said, "Well, God, I thought you wanted me to form this institute. I have been following Your lead for so long. But why have you abandoned me now? I am all alone again."

But again, the question simply repeats itself: What are you doing here, Eric? I calmed down and tried to answer this question. I said, "I am here to share what I've learned over the years in building faithful inclusive community and to empower more and more people to do this work in more and more places." With this, I knew I was not here to re-create an old program that had worked before. I was able to let go of the old paradigm that made the Kaleidoscope Project a success, which included commitment and support of the dioceses and conferences with which I had contractual agreements. With this new institute, I did not have the explicit support of the church institutions. I had to find another way to connect with local church communities and leaders. I knew what I needed to do.

I spent a month listening to local church leaders to find out what their needs were. Based on the listening, I was free to re-vision the Institute based on the needs of the church communities that I was trying to serve. Then I called a meeting, inviting people whom I had trained in programs of the last five years. I presented this new vision to them, and they were excited, agreeing that the Institute would be a success. In August 2006, we had our first Kaleidoscope Summer Training Institute. We envisioned an event for twenty-five people. We were thrilled to have over thirty-five participants from five states and five Christian denominations. On the last day, we commissioned over fifteen people who had made a commitment to become trainers for the Institute—learning the skills, models, theories, and theology of this ministry and becoming proficient in sharing this ministry with more local church communities.

Again, the question, "What are you doing here?" was the key for me to face my fear, moving me from being alone to forming a community of trust. The question refocused my energy away from worry, anxiety, and fear and toward reclaiming what God was calling me to be. I was called to anoint others, building a community of the faithful, to continue the ministry of God.

I arrived at a city in the South to do a twelve-hour workshop for a major Christian denomination. Peter, who was my contact up to this point, picked me up at the airport. As he drove me to my first meeting with the staff at the denominational office, he said, "You're in for a real challenge." I sensed fear coming from him—perhaps fear for my safety. For most events, I usually arrived late the day before or on the day of the workshop. This time, Peter insisted that I be here a full day earlier to meet with the "key players." With a few probing questions from me, he shared that, as a White male who was advocating for a workshop on multicultural ministry, he had received very negative feedback from both the African American and European American leaders. He had encountered resistance from all sides, and ownership to this program was low.

My fear meter went up a few degrees as I listened. What have I gotten myself into? I was entering into an unknown environment with people with whom I had no relationship or preestablished trust. I should be afraid. But I said to myself, "Practice what you preach, Eric. Create a trustful environment; help them get to know you, then you should be okay." That was my mental preparation before I entered into the first meeting. Complication! The leader of the group was delayed. I was not in position to suggest affirming a set of Respectful Communication Guidelines. As we waited, people started talking. I knew this meeting was getting off on the "wrong foot." Almost immediately, the group went into a familiar destructive ritual—an African American spoke in very forceful way that doing a "multicultural ministry" workshop was just another way of ignoring the issues of the African Americans in the South. Besides, what could a person from California know about our issues? The ritual continued with the rest of the group not able to challenge his blatant assumptions of me, though I was sitting right there. Instead, they sat in silent guilt. In my anxious silence, I knew I couldn't count on anyone there to support me. My fear meter went up a few more degrees. I felt alone.

What Am I Doing Here?

Ten years ago, I would have become defensive and launched an aggressive counterattack upon the ones who belittled me. Instead, I stayed silent and observed the group interactions and, more importantly, what was going on inside me. I asked myself: What does this fear reveal about me? I quickly recalled how the issues I faced as a Chinese American were often ignored and trivialized when I participated in anti-racism workshops back in the 1980s. During one such workshop at a seminary, after the Black and White panel finished sharing their perspectives on racism, I got up and spoke about the issue from a Chinese immigrant's perspective. I basically said something like, "As we move forward to address the issue of racism, don't forget there are minorities of other races besides African Americans." The response from one of the African Americans on the panel was: "If you want to be on the panel, why don't you speak up? We can't read minds." The European Americans responded: "We are so glad that you are finally claiming your racial identity."

Twenty-five years later this fear I had of being rejected and belittled was being triggered again. If I had gone on the counter-attack, I would have replayed the same ritual that played itself out twenty-five years ago. Then the familiar question came, "What are you doing here, Eric?" And I answered, "I am here not to replay old ritual that escalates more fear and hurts. I am here to build bridges across misunderstandings. I am here to build trust and share what I've learned."

While I was arriving at the above conclusion, the group around the table was playing out another ritual. Consciously or unconsciously, those who had power in this context simply allowed the division and competition among the "minorities" to continue. As long as they were fighting over what to call this workshop and who was supposed to know the real issue of racism, the powerful did not have to do anything or face their own fears. How could I keep myself from being dragged into this ritual? As their consultant, how could I help this group to step out of the unhelpful ritual and move into a more productive, faithful approach to the issue? How could I not be the fear-bearer or fear-conqueror? How could I expose the fear-exploiters' scheme to destroy the possibility of intimacy in this situation?

The leader of the group finally arrived. I took that as an opportunity to ask the group to introduce themselves so that I would know who they were. The person to my right began her introduction. As they went around the room, I listened. Finally, it was my turn. My instinct said to me that they needed to know who I was, not what I could do. I opened my mouth and found myself telling my story as an immigrant coming to the United States in 1970. The first stop was Augusta, Georgia, where my aunt lived. I sensed the group was a little surprised. I spoke about how I reacted to the brand of racism in the Deep South. Then I moved on to sharing my experiences moving to New York City, going to a multiracial school, living in a multicultural community. I shared my experience of multicultural living at Cornell, the intercultural issues I encountered in Seminary in Boston, my first job as a priest at the University of Southern California, and how I got into this ministry of building inclusive community by teaching at the School of Education there and being active in AIDS education. I shared how, after the 1992 Los Angeles Riots, I created dialogue programs on racial reconciliation for people from nine major religions. I concluded by saying two key things:

1. I admitted that I did not know the African American experience, especially in the South, but I was here to share what I knew hoping that what I would share would be helpful.
2. People who did diversity and multicultural workshops and did not address racism from a Black/White perspective in the United States were not doing their jobs. In another setting, the Black/White dynamics/history may not be as pertinent. But doing a diversity workshop in the South, addressing the Black/White issues had to be an essential part of the program.

As I spoke, I made connection with each one of them based on their sharing. To connect with the African American, I shared my reflection on "A Day without Immigrants Protest" that had occurred the week before across the United States. Los Angeles had had one of the biggest turnouts and had gotten a lot of coverage. I used the opportunity to talk about how the media and the politicians were trying to use the divide-and-conquer technique again to divert people's attention away from the real issues—the joblessness rate in Mexico and the United States employers' exploitation of these workers by hiring them at below a living wage, while claiming that they did not have any rights because they were "illegal." Instead, the media and politicians were projecting the issue as the illegal immigrants taking away jobs from African Americans and other struggling low-income families. As long as the illegal immigrants and the minority and low-income citizens were fighting over who was taking whose jobs, we remained distracted from addressing the fear-exploiters' political and financial gains. As this community moved forward in the work of dismantling racism and building multicultural inclusive community, we had to resist being sucked into this divide-and-conquer pattern.

As I responded to the person who suggested that most people in the region were in denial about racism, I launched into a description of the stages of intercultural sensitivity.[2] I said, "First, we have to expose those who are in denial to people who are different. Then if they are truly in denial, they will react defensively. This defensive

[2]See Milton J. Bennett, "A Developmental Approach to Training for Inter-cultural Sensitivity," in *Theories and Methods in Cross-Cultural Orientation*, ed. Judith N. Martin, International Journal of Intercultural Relations, vol. 5, no. 2 (New York/Oxford/Beijing/Frankfurt/Sao Paulo/Sydney/Tokyo/Toronto: Per-gamon Press, 1986), 179–96. I also described these stages in Eric H. F. Law, *The Bush Was Blazing But Not Consumed* (St. Louis: Chalice Press, 1996), 46–60.

posture is actually an improvement from denial because they are at least aware that there are people who are different." In doing so, I affirmed the good work that Peter had done by coordinating the workshop and stated that people's defensive reactions were actually a sign of progress.

I continued, "We then need to help people in the defensive stage to get to know their own culture by doing intragroup dialogue processes. Then engaging them in intergroup dialogue would be the next step. Then they might move to the next stage, in which they would say differences are not important and that sharing what we have in common is the way." I explained how this stage was not productive and that they needed to provide educational programs to help people to move toward acceptance of differences. By this time the African American who implied that I could not know or understand his issues was taking notes.

A childish part of me said I was vindicated. But this involved more than being vindicated. I had achieved a little intimacy with him and with this group of people who did not know me or trust me an hour before. Ultimately, it was my trust in God that got me through this fearful experience. It was God's question, "What are you doing here?" that helped me focus and live through this fear. A part of me knew that God, through Christ's ministry, invited me to stand up and be the prophetic voice since I was perceived by some in the room as a powerless person. Another part of me knew that God, through Christ, invited the powerful side of me (in this case, I was the expert, brought in to give this workshop) to take up the cross and let go of my ego. I decided to do both. My actions in declaring that I did not claim to know the experience of African American was my willingness to take up the cross. At the same time, my faith in God also empowered me to speak the truth about myself, which began with my knowledge of myself—my fear, my gifts, and my abilities. As they knew more about me and as they realized how I had listened to them and attempted to connect with them, trust began to build. This group of people became my allies the next day when I facilitated the workshop. Through their verbal support and their comfort-giving posture throughout the day, participants, who were apprehensive about coming to the workshop, felt more at ease and were able to participate more fully in the dialogue and learning processes. I was not alone.

"What are you doing here?" This is the question I ask myself before every speech, every workshop and training program that

I give. Believe it or not, I still have fear before I get up and speak. The moment I think I am fully prepared, and have no fear, I am not taking my audience seriously because every audience is different with different contexts, experiences, interests, and needs. Having this fear is actually a gift. The way to focus my energy and live through this fear is to ask: What am I doing here?

This is the question that God asked Elijah when he was fearful. Like Elijah, we will go through stormy emotions as we run away from our fear. But, eventually, we have to find that quiet place, the sound of sheer silence, the still small voice that is the voice of the Holy. This is the place where we become intimate with God. Here, we will hear the question echo again: What are you doing here? When we can answer that question, we recapture our relationship with God. We reclaim our status as children of God. And God clarifies our call to ministry. Then, we are ready to go back to do what we are called to do. In doing so, we will empower others to work with us in community. In the trust and intimacy of community, we will be able to face and work through any fear that comes our way. We are not alone.

Questions and Activities

1. This chapter included three examples of how the author worked through his fears to achieve intimacy by answering the question: "What are you doing here?" Try this the next time you are facing a fearful situation.
    a. Name a fearful situation.
    b. Answer this question: What am I doing here?
    c. Take time to be silent. Write down what emerges from your silence.
    d. Then ask the question again: What am I doing here?
    e. Spend a little more time in silence. Write down what transpired in the silence.
    f. Then ask the question again: What am I doing here? Silence.
    g. Write down again any new insight that comes to you.

8

I Need Your Light

When darkness overcomes this land,
And I can hardly see to reach for your hand,
I need your light; I need your light.

When gloomy shadows shroud our hearts,
Dividing friends with fears that tear us apart,
I need your light; I need your light.

I need your light to shine and burst through the clouds of fears
and lies.
I need your light to light a rainbow of truth across the skies.
I need your light; I need your light.

When bullying supplants debate,
When patriotic means to advocate hate,
I need your light; I need your light.

When fear becomes the air we breathe,
When lies are told as truths for us to believe,
I need your light; I need your light.

I need your light to find my courage to touch and love my foes.
I need your light to lift my burden so I can fly and glow.
So I'll be the light
as you are the light.

We'll be the light to light the pathway to justice, truth, and
grace.
Let's be the lights to clear the shadows and make an open space.
Where we are free

Where we can speak our truth
Where we can fly and shine and burst through the clouds of
fears and lies.
Let's be the light to light the rainbow of truth across the skies.
Let's be the light.
Let's be the light.
Let's be the light.

I wrote this song in April of 2017 to express my need for others to be the light with me in a world darkened by fears. How can we "make an open space where we are free, where we can speak our truth" when "fear becomes the air we breathe"?

Look Deeply in Your Fear

Vietnamese Buddhist monk and peace activist Thich Nhat Hanh, in his book *FEAR: Essential Wisdom for Getting Through the Storm*, said, "The only way to ease our fear and be truly happy is to acknowledge our fear and look deeply at its source."[1] He also said, "Fear keeps us focused on the past or worried about the future. If we can acknowledge our fear, we can realize that right now we are okay. Right now, today, we are still alive and our bodies are working marvelously. Our eyes can still see the beautiful sky. Our ears can still hear the voices of our loved ones."[2] He prescribes the practice of five remembrances in order for us to look deeply into the nature and roots of our fear. He invites us to breathe slowly and mindfully, in and out, deep and slow, while we say these remembrances to ourselves:

1. I am of the nature to grow old. I cannot escape growing old.
2. I am of the nature to have ill health. I cannot escape having ill health.
3. I am of the nature to die. I cannot escape death.
4. All that is dear to me, and everyone I love, are of the nature to change. There is no way to escape being separated from them.
5. I inherit the results of my acts of body, speech, and mind. My actions are my continuation.[3]

---

[1]Thich Nhat Hanh, *Fear: Essential Wisdom for Getting Through the Storm* (New York: HarperCollins, 2012), 1.

[2]Ibid., 4.

[3]Ibid., 29–30.

For me, these are truth statements about being human. Acknowledging these truths puts fear in its place. If fear has become the air we breathe, causing us to alienate ourselves from self and others, then why not breathe in the truth about that which we fear the most, mindfully and deeply, in order to mine from it wisdom, courage, serenity, and even joy?

Fear in the Social Media Age

One example of fear-arousing news in 2016 was the alleged Russian meddling in the presidential election through the Internet and social media. Facebook believed that 120 fake Russian-backed profile pages created 80,000 posts that were received by 29 million Americans directly. These posts had the potential to reach as many as 126 million by users sharing, liking, and following them. Google said it had discovered thousands of dollars' worth of ads with suspicious Russian ties, as well as eighteen YouTube channels linked to the Kremlin's disinformation campaign. Twitter found 2,752 accounts linked to Russian operatives.[4]

As for the content of these ads, emails, and posts, they targeted different cross sections of the U.S. population and citizens at opposite sides of the political spectrum with exaggerated and false information to propagate fear of the others and of a particular candidate. An example of an ad shows a picture of Jesus arm-wrestling with Satan, and the captions said, "Satan: If I win, Clinton wins! Jesus: Not if I can help it!"[5]

Social media and the Internet are revolutionary in the sense that they connect people across the globe and provide speedy access to information in a way that we have never seen before. But along with their benefits to human communities, we are seeing the dark side of how these tools are being used to propagate fears. They also isolate people from interpersonal face-to-face interactions while offering the illusion of, and substitute for, intimacy. These media also allow individuals to select friends and choose content to the extent that they may never see anything that another group or individual with different preferences would see. A case in point: I never saw any of the divisive Russian ads until I decided to do a search on Google.

[4]Olivia Solon and Sabrina Siddiqui, "Russia-backed Facebook posts reached 126M Americans during US election," *The Guardian,* October 30, 2017, https://www.theguardian.com/technology/2017/oct/30/facebook-russia-fake-accounts-126-million .
[5]Ibid.

Enough said about the danger of social media, with its immense power to reach millions of people almost instantaneously. Let's talk about how we can use the same media for addressing fears constructively by spreading truth and facilitating human contacts and communities. As a reaction to the defeat of the first viable female presidential candidate, Teresa Shook of Hawaii created a Facebook event and invited friends to march on Washington in protest. Similar Facebook pages were created by others and quickly led to thousands of women signing up to march. They decided to unite their efforts and consolidate their pages, thus the beginning of the official organization of the Women's March on Washington. Less than three months later, in January of 2017, between 440,000 to 500,000 people showed up at the Women's March on Washington. Across the United States, somewhere between 3,267,134 and 5,246,670 people participated in 408 local marches. In total, worldwide participation has been estimated at over five million. Reportedly, 673 marches took place worldwide, on all seven continents. The Washington March was streamed live on YouTube, Facebook, and Twitter.[6]

The Women's March was real proof that we can use social media effectively to form communities and to speak truth together. Two other movements that used social media effectively to speak the truth are #blacklivesmatter and #metoo. For me, these movements are about fear-bearers connecting through social media, forming communities of resistance. Social media became a starting place for fear-bearers to stand up and say that they will not buy into the fear-exploiters' plots any more. Time and again we hear women finding the courage to speak their truth because they saw others in their networks doing so. We should educate ourselves about how to use social media and the Internet for spreading truth and forming communities.

Waves of Truth

The week after the 2017 presidential inauguration, I started the #3MillionTruth movement. I did this after President Trump accused three million people of voting illegally, citing his claim as the reason he lost the popular vote. Before and after the 2016 election, individuals and groups used Twitter, Facebook, and Instagram to propagate false claims, half-truths, and lies resulting

[6]"2017 Women's March," Wikipedia, https://en.wikipedia.org/wiki/2017_Women%27s_March

in millions of people believing these false claims, fake facts, and made-up stories as truth. Meanwhile the traditional mainstream media were made to look like fools, constantly being referred to as "fake news." I proposed the #3MillionTruth movement as a way to counter these waves of untruth.

I proposed that we create a network of at least three million people who would take thirty seconds a day to post the truth on Twitter, Facebook, and Instagram whenever we encountered a lie coming from individuals and groups who seek to divide and distract us. Soon after I started the movement, someone asked, "What's the use? Is it going to change anything?" My response was: some people have millions of followers on Twitter. Every time they tweet a lie, that many people may see and believe it. The only way to counter a lie is with the truth. In the case of the Internet, we have to counter the lie with the truth plus volumes. If we are successful in getting three million people to tell the truth, their followers and friends will see it. If ten friends/followers of the three million get their messages of truth, we would have touched 30 million people. Think of it as a wave of truth that can wash away the lie. We talk about people surfing the Internet. I hope that they will surf the wave of truth that we create through #3milliontruth.

In order for this to work, we need to make a commitment to tweet and post truth every time we see and hear a lie on the Internet. There are different orders of truth.[7]

1. *Factual Truth* is based on observable physical evidence. If you have the facts and evidence about an issue and topic, please post them, because factual truth always trumps the other orders of truth. However, before you post something as factual truth, check out its source and verify its accuracy. There are way too many fake facts out there.

2. *Interpreted Truth* is based on an individual's or group's interpretation of the event. This kind of truth is often up for debate because there are always different interpretations. Throughout history, the powerful always take their interpreted truth and make it *the* truth, and then expect everyone else to believe it. Trump's claim that there were three million illegal voters was an interpreted truth. We have to counter this "interpretation" with factual truth and experienced truth.

[7]I first described these different kinds of truth in Eric H. F. Law, *The Word at the Crossings* (St. Louis: Chalice Press, 2004), 54–55.

3. *Experienced Truth* is based on one's own experience of the event, topic, and issue. This is the truth I invite people to post. For example, I have asked people to post the truth of their voting experiences in this form:

> "I am a US citizen; I voted (or did not vote) for _____ and I saw no illegal voting activities at the last election."

If three million people post their truth, that means we have three million pairs of eyes and ears noticing that there were no illegal voting activities. On the other hand, these same three million pairs of eyes and ears may also notice and report real incidents of voter suppression activities—seeing people being turned away from polls, lack of polling locations, people in poor neighborhoods having to wait hours to vote. This wave of experienced truth can call into question false claims, and may change the minds of those who believe them if our wave of truth is big enough to reach them.

A week after I started the #3MillionTruth movement, over 1,000 people participated in creating a little wave of truth. That was not bad, but it was nowhere near the goal of three million people. I am sad to report that it did not go much further from there. So here is what I suggest we do to try again:

1. Use #3MillionTruth every time you post your experienced truth and the factual truth to counter a lie that you notice.
2. Use a second hashtag beginning with #TruthAbout . . . to indicate a more specific topic for which you are telling the factual and experience truth. For example:
   — The U.S. government already thoroughly screens refugees' backgrounds—an intensive process involving the Department of Homeland Security, the FBI, and the national intelligence agencies. The process takes eighteen to twenty-four months. #3MillionTruth #TruthAboutRefugees
3. Add a line at the end of your post to invite your followers and friends to post their experienced and factual truth. For example:
   — A colleague of mine is an undocumented immigrant. She was brought to the U.S. when she was very young. She did well in school, works hard, and pays taxes. She has never committed any crime #3MillionTruth #TruthAboutImmigrants. Every time you hear a lie, tweet and post your experienced truth. Do it.

— Mexicans made up only 52 percent of all undocumented immigrants according to the Pew Research Center. So building the Southern Border wall will not stop the other 48 percent #3MillionTruth #TruthAboutTheBorderWall. If you know of other factual truth, tweet it, post it, Instagram it, now.

4. Retweet and share posts that you believe reflect your experienced truth with your friends and followers. On Twitter, you can tweet the same message as many times as you want. The more we do this using hashtags (like #3MillionTruth), the more we can increase the reach and popularity (trending) of our hashtags and messages. Remember, we are aiming for waves of three million people to post their truths.

So let us go forth and make more waves of truth.

What Americans Fear

Beginning in 2014, Chapman University in Orange, California, initiated an annual nationwide poll on what strikes fear in Americans. In the 2015 survey[8], which included 1,500 participants from across the United States and all walks of life, the top ten things Americans feared the most were:

- Corruption of government officials
- Cyber-terrorism
- Corporate tracking of personal information
- Terrorist attacks
- Government tracking of personal information
- Biowarfare
- Identity theft
- Economic collapse
- Running out of money in the future
- Credit card fraud

In 2016, the survey[9] showed that the top ten fears were:

- Corrupt government officials
- Terrorist attacks
- Not having enough money for the future
- Terrorism

---

[8]Sheri Ledbetter, "America's Top Fears 2015," Chapman University, October 13, 2015, https://blogs.chapman.edu/wilkinson/2015/10/13/americas-top-fears-2015/.

[9]"America's Top Fears 2016," Chapman University, October 11, 2016, https://blogs.chapman.edu/wilkinson/2016/10/11/americas-top-fears-2016/ .

- Government restrictions on firearms and ammunition
- People I love dying
- Economic/financial collapse
- Identity theft
- People I love becoming seriously ill
- The Affordable Care Act/Obamacare

The result of the 2017 survey[10] show that the top ten fears were:

- Corrupt government officials
- American Health Care Act/Trumpcare
- Pollution of oceans, rivers and lakes
- Pollution of drinking water
- Not having enough money for the future
- High medical bills
- The U.S. being involved in another World War
- Global warming and climate change
- North Korea using nuclear weapons
- Air pollution

I wonder what caused the fear of "corrupt government officials" being the thing that American feared the most for three years in a row? Who stands to gain from propagating this fear of government officials? Who are the fear-exploiters here? The analysis of the 2015 survey shed light on my wonderment:

"The researchers asked respondents if they had engaged in particular actions because of their fears. What they learned is nearly a fourth of Americans report having voted for a particular candidate due to their fears; and more than 10 percent have purchased a gun due to fear. Other behaviors driven by fear are sending kids to private schools and purchasing a home alarm system."[11] "Fear of the government had the strongest relationship with buying a gun because of fear," said L. Edward Day, Ph.D., the lead researcher on this portion of the survey. "People who have purchased a gun because of fear also have high levels of fear of technology and crime."[12]

---

[10]"America's Top Fears 2017," Chapman University, October 11, 2017, https://blogs.chapman.edu/wilkinson/2017/10/11/americas-top-fears-2017/

[11]Sheri Ledbetter, "Americans Fear Most – Chapman University's second annual Survey of American Fears released," Chapman University, October 13, 2015, https://blogs.chapman.edu/press-room/2015/10/13/what-americans-fear-most-chapman-universitys-second-annual-survey-of-american-fears-released/ .

[12]Ibid.

The year 2016 was a presidential election year. Of course both political parties were using fear to get votes. Notice the 2015 survey result revealed fears concerning technology, terrorism, and finance. In 2016, healthcare issues became three of the top ten fears, and gun restriction entered the top ten as well. I wonder why neither of these fears appeared in the 2015 survey result?

With President Trump in office, the top fears in 2017 again shifted. This time environmental issues took up four of the top ten spots, and the fear of the U.S. becoming involved in wars took up two spots. Terrorism actually did not make it into the top ten, and gun restriction also disappeared.

While the fear of corrupt government officials and economic concerns are consistent throughout the years, I would invite my readers to reflect on their personal experiences and try to explain the shifts across three short years in what and whom we fear. I have created charts for both 2016 and 2017 for you to analyze these fears yourselves. For each fear, I invite you to reflect on four questions:

— What changes or events in the U.S. caused this fear to rise to the top?
— Who and what groups were naming or propagating this fear?
— What did this fear cause you and/or others to do, if anything?
— Who and what groups stand to gain from people acting on this fear?

Assuming Chapman University will continue to do this survey year after year, you can do this reflection every year. Below (p.109) is a three-year comparison including 2018. I have included the actual percentage of respondents who voted for each of the fears. The fears around the concerns of environment continue to increase in the second year of the Trump's presidency. Judging from the increase in percentage of respondents' votes on the top fears, "Americans are becoming more afraid."[13]

---

[13]America's Top Fears 2018, Chapman University Survey of American Fears, October 16, 2018, https://blogs.chapman.edu/wilkinson/2018/10/16/americas-top-fears-2018/ .

2016 Top Ten Fears	What changes or events in the U.S. caused this fear to rise to the top?	Who and what groups were naming or propagating this fear?	What did this fear cause you and/or others to do if anything?	Who and what groups stand to gain from people acting on this fear?
Corrupt government officials				
Terrorist attack				
Not having enough money for the future				
Terrorism				
Government restrictions on firearms and ammunition				
People I love dying				
Economic/ financial collapse				
Identity theft				
People I love becoming seriously ill				
The Affordable Care Act/ Obamacare				

2017 Top Ten Fears	What changes or events in the U.S. caused this fear to rise to the top?	Who and what groups were naming or propagating this fear?	What did this fear cause you and/or others to do if anything?	Who and what groups stand to gain from people acting on this fear?
Corrupt government officials				
American Health Care Act/Trumpcare				
Pollution of oceans, rivers and lakes				
Pollution of drinking water				
Not having enough money for the future				
High medical bills				
The U.S. getting involved in another World War				
Global warming and climate change				
North Korea using nuclear weapons				
Air pollution				

Top Ten Fears (2016-2018)[14]

	2016	2017	2018
1.	Corrupt government officials (60.6%)	Corrupt government officials (74.5%)	Corrupt government officials (73.6%)
2.	Terrorist attack (41%)	American Healthcare Act/Trumpcare (55.3%)	Pollution of oceans, rivers, and lakes (61.6%)
3.	Not having enough money for the future (39.9%)	Pollution of oceans, rivers, and lakes (53.1%)	Pollution of drinking water (60.7%)
4.	Terrorism (38.5%)	Pollution of drinking water (50.4%)	Not having enough money for the future (57%)
5.	Gun control (38.5%)	Not having enough money for the future (50.2%)	People I love becoming seriously ill (56.5%)
6.	People I love dying (38.1%)	High medical bills (48.4%)	People I love dying (56.4%)
7.	Economic/financial collapse (37.5%)	The U.S. getting involved in another World War (48.4%)	Air pollution (55.1%)
8.	Identity theft (37.1%)	Global warming & climate change (48%)	Extinction of plant and animal species (54.1%)
9.	People I love becoming seriously ill (35.9%)	North Korea using nuclear weapons (47.5%)	Global warming and climate change (53.2%)
10.	The Affordable Health Care Act/Obamacare (35.5%)	Air pollution (44.9%)	High medical bills (52.9%)

Given the increase in the frequency of natural disasters in the last two years, I wonder why the fear of natural disasters is not in the top ten fears. I went back to look at the original surveys and discovered that natural disaster was one of the ten domains of fears, which included earthquakes, tornados, droughts, floods, and hurricanes! None of these fears had gained more than 35% in the last three years, and in 2018, drought is ranked at 34, tornado at 39, hurricane at 43, flood at 46, and earthquake at 47. I wonder why fear of these phenomena, which present more imminent danger, are not in the consciousness of the U.S. population. I wonder who stands to gain from people not taking the fear of natural disaster seriously? I will reflect on this further later in this chapter.

[14]Ibid.

Putting Fear in Its Place

In his book *Following Jesus in a Culture of Fear*, Christian ethicist and moral theologian Scott Bader-Saye shared a set of diagnostic questions that I found helpful: [15]

- Is this thing you fear actually present or fast-approaching? Or is it far off, either in terms of distance (like a tornado that's a hundred miles away), time (like something that won't likely happen for years), or likelihood (like something that happens to one out of a million people)?
- Is the thing you fear really powerful and able to cause you harm? Or is it something that is generally small and harmless?
- Is the thing that you fear really a threat? That is, will it really cause you to lose something you love, or does it just seem scary because it is strange?
- Are you afraid of losing something that is of real importance? Or is that "something" a thing that you shouldn't be so concerned about in the first place?
- Do you fear so much that you are closing in on yourself or unjustly lashing out at others?
- Does your fear keep you from doing things you know you should do?
- Does your fear take away the joy you feel in the presence of things you love (like your family) because you are afraid of losing them?
- Is your fear the result of someone's attempt to manipulate you? Is anyone profiting from your fearfulness (like a business getting your money, a politician getting your vote, or a religious leader getting your offering)?

For the first question, I have created an analytical chart for you to rate the top ten fears of 2018. You are invited to name more specifically the person or things that you fear by answering the first two questions:

— Whom or what do you fear?
— What personal harm or loss for you and/or your loved ones might this fear present?

Then you are invited to rate each fear using two scales. The "how-soon" scale helps you determine your level of active

---

[15]Scott Bader-Saye, *Following Jesus in a Culture of Fear* (Michigan: Brazos Press, 2007), 60–61.

engagement to address this fear. The "likelihood" scale helps you determine how real this threat is. If you rate a particular fear as immediate (5) and almost certain (5) that it will happen to you, then you must spring into action to avoid and alleviate this danger. For example, if you are in a movie theater and someone yells "FIRE" and the fire alarm is ringing, the fear of dying in a fire is immediate and very likely to happen. So you should take action quickly to get out and to help others to get out of the theater.

If you rate a fear as immediate or within weeks (5-4) but it is unlikely and rare (1-2) that it would happen to you, then you can remind yourself that you are not in danger and can use your resources to help others who might be in immediate danger. For example, if I have a fear of hurricanes, and a hurricane is about to hit 1,000 miles away, I don't need to go to a storm shelter to protect myself, but can use my connections and resources to support those who are facing the imminent disaster.

If you rate a fear as years or a long way away (1-2) but it is almost certain or very likely (5-4) that it will happen, then you have time to work on changing the outcome. For example, I might have the fear that our water and air are being polluted, which will most likely (4) happen if we don't do anything to reverse the trend. However, we may not feel and see the impact on our lives until years (2) from now. I can take this year to work toward changing community and government policies to reverse the trend of pollution.

If you rate a fear as "a long way away" (1) and unlikely and rare (1-2), then you don't have to act immediately and you can take time to explore why this fear was triggered in you and by whom. Perhaps this fear was used by the marketers and fear-exploiters to get your money or your vote.

2018 Top Ten Fears	Whom or what do you fear?	What personal harm or loss for you and/ or your loved ones might this fear present?	On a scale of 1 to 5, how imminent is the harm and danger presented by this fear?				
Corrupt govt. officials			Imme-diate **5**	Week **4**	Month **3**	Year **2**	Long way away **1**
			Almost certain **5**	Likely **4**	Possi-ble **3**	Un-likely **2**	Rare **1**
Pollution of oceans, rivers, and lakes			Imme-diate **5**	Week **4**	Month **3**	Year **2**	Long way away **1**
			Almost certain **5**	Likely **4**	Possi-ble **3**	Un-likely **2**	Rare **1**
Pollution of drinking water			Imme-diate **5**	Week **4**	Month **3**	Year **2**	Long way away **1**
			Almost certain **5**	Likely **4**	Possi-ble **3**	Un-likely **2**	Rare **1**
Not having enough money for the future			Imme-diate **5**	Week **4**	Month **3**	Year **2**	Long way away **1**
			Almost certain **5**	Likely **4**	Possi-ble **3**	Un-likely **2**	Rare **1**
People I love becoming seriously ill			Imme-diate **5**	Week **4**	Month **3**	Year **2**	Long way away **1**
			Almost certain **5**	Likely **4**	Possi-ble **3**	Un-likely **2**	Rare **1**

People I love dying			Imme-diate **5**	Week **4**	Month **3**	Year **2**	Long way away **1**
			Almost certain **5**	Likely **4**	Possi-ble **3**	Un-likely **2**	Rare **1**
Air Pollution			Imme-diate **5**	Week **4**	Month **3**	Year **2**	Long way away **1**
			Almost certain **5**	Likely **4**	Possi-ble **3**	Un-likely **2**	Rare **1**
Extinction of plant and animal species			Imme-diate **5**	Week **4**	Month **3**	Year **2**	Long way away **1**
			Almost certain **5**	Likely **4**	Possi-ble **3**	Un-likely **2**	Rare **1**
Global warming and climate change			Imme-diate **5**	Week **4**	Month **3**	Year **2**	Long way away **1**
			Almost certain **5**	Likely **4**	Possi-ble **3**	Un-likely **2**	Rare **1**
High medical bills			Imme-diate **5**	Week **4**	Month **3**	Year **2**	Long way away **1**
			Almost certain **5**	Likely **4**	Possi-ble **3**	Un-likely **2**	Rare **1**

If you need help with the "likelihood" scale rating, review chapter 1, where I shared the discipline of linking a fear to the high-stakes or worst-case destination as a way to determine whether the danger is imminent.

During the 2016 election season, I wrote a blog post using this discipline to evaluate two fears propagated by the two candidates: Fear of Clinton taking away our guns and fear of Trump starting World War III. When I wrote the blog post, I didn't know who was going to be elected president.

First case: Donald Trump said that if you voted for Clinton, she would take away your guns. When I tried to link this to its most terrible outcome, here was what I came up with: When

Clinton becomes President, she will nominate a Supreme Court Justice who is anti-gun. Congress then approves this nomination. When a gun rights case reaches the Supreme Court, the majority of justices will vote in favor of it and we will begin to lose our right to bear arms. Eventually Clinton will get Congress to amend the Second Amendment or get rid of it altogether. When my guns are taken away, I will be without protection. So when I am at work, or at a public place, or even in my own home, if there is a shooting, I am dead.

In this scenario, there are many steps in between Clinton getting elected as President and my getting killed because I don't have my gun to protect myself. I would rate this fear using the two scales as years away (2) and unlikely to happen (2). This should calm me down a bit because the imminent danger is not there and now I can do something about this fear. Then we can look at this in a wider context. Why then do I have this fear of not being able to carry a gun? When I am able to identify my real concern, I might be able to do something constructive to address it. Perhaps it has nothing to do with whom I vote for in the upcoming election. Maybe I should be doing something locally or in my neighborhood to foster safety for the whole community.

Second case: Hillary Clinton said that if you voted for Trump, he would have access to nuclear weapons and start World War III. Let's use the same technique and link this to its most terrible outcome. When Trump becomes President, he will have direct access to deploy nuclear arms. When another head of state says something about him that he considers a putdown, he reacts in a "strong" way and calls for a nuclear attack. His military advisors warn him not to act so impulsively but he calls them "losers" and fires them. So he "pushes the button" and creates mass destruction, and the other nation retaliates and sends nuclear arms our way, and I die.

Now with any other candidate for President, this scenario sounds a little ridiculous. I would have rated this fear as something that may happen within a few years (2) and it is unlikely and rare (1-2). But with Trump, given what we knew about him and his temperament then and what we know now, this scenario, for me, was not that far-fetched At that time, I believed that the distance was very short between Trump getting elected and his using nuclear arms, resulting in my death and the deaths of countless others. . I would have rated this fear as something that is possible (3) and can happen within months (3). This, to me, constituted a more imminent danger, and I felt the need to act on this because Trump was literally only a few votes away from becoming the President.

And he did win the election. In 2017, the first year of the Trump presidency, we witnessed this scenario playing out with North Korea. No wonder the fear of entering into World War III and war with North Korea became part of the top ten fears. In Trump's first State of the Union address, he said he wanted the U.S. to build more nuclear bombs!

Clinton, during her campaign, also asserted that if Trump won, we would be undoing the gains we made on civil rights and the environment. Today, we are seeing these things coming true. Yet people in many states responded to the fear of Clinton more than the fear of Trump, giving Trump the electoral votes. I was puzzled by the election result because by my analysis, the things I feared about a Trump presidency were more imminent than those associated with a Clinton presidency. Winning an election seems to be about who can make more people fear the other candidate, not about telling the truth. Why did some fears cause more people to act, despite the fact that the danger was not imminent, while other fears based on imminent and real threats did not get people to address them?

Fear and Truth

As I was putting together the analytical charts, I realized that most people do not go about addressing their fears in an intellectual and analytical way. All these charts and questions are for getting at the truth—the truth of how real a fear might be—which then informs how to address it. But observing what was happening between 2016 and 2018, I noticed that truth did not seem to matter to many people. And our highest government officials were not helping by calling the news reports that they did not like, "fake news." Yet truth is one of the most important remedies for alleviating our fear. This is precisely why the fear-exploiters of our time do not want truth to be told and heard by people whom they want to manipulate.

The 2014 Chapman University fear survey showed that a majority of Americans believed crimes such as child abduction and gang violence had increased over the previous twenty years. Dr. Edward Day, who led the research and analysis of the survey, reported, "When we looked at statistical data from police and FBI records, it showed crime has actually *decreased* in America in the past twenty years. Criminologists often get angry responses when we try to tell people the crime rate has gone down."[16]

In the 2016 survey, the researchers made up a story called "the North Dakota crash" and asked the respondents whether they believed the government had covered that up. Nearly one-third of the respondents believed that![17]

In the same survey, the researchers learned that more than half of respondents (63 percent) believed that "natural disasters in my area are capable of doing serious harm to me or my property." The vast majority (78 percent) believed an emergency kit would improve their chances of surviving a disaster. Nevertheless, 74 percent had made no effort to put together such a kit.[18]

I am baffled. Even in the face of self-admitted truth, three-fourths of Americans still do no take action to lower their risk. Fear of natural disaster did not even make the top ten fears for the three years of the Chapman University fear survey. I live in Southern California, I would rate natural disaster such as an earthquake as something that could happen any time, perhaps in weeks (4) and it is most certain that it will hit (5). Who is controlling what we should fear? Who stands to gain from making us fear the wrong thing and ignore the real fear of imminent danger that we can do something about?

Different Fear for Different Folks

In 2017, a week after Hurricane Harvey hit Texas, I was visiting a relative in Lake Arrowhead, located in the San Bernardino Mountains in Southern California. Across from my relative's home was a house surrounded by heavy wrought iron fences. Right behind the gate was a huge sign that said, "Liberal Free Zone." Flying in front of the house was a large American flag. My immediate reaction was "Oh, I'm not welcomed in that house. But how would they

---

[16]Sheri Ledbetter, "What Americans Fear Most – New Poll from Chapman University," Chapman University, October 20, 2014, https://blogs.chapman.edu/press-room/2014/10/20/what-americans-fear-most-new-poll-from-chapman-university/ .

[17]"What Aren't They Telling Us? Chapman University Survey of American Fears," Chapman University, October 11, 2016, https://blogs.chapman.edu/wilkinson/2016/10/11/what-arent-they-telling-us/ .

[18]Sheri Ledbetter, "What do Americans Fear Most? Chapman University's Third Annual Survey of American Fears Released," Chapman University, October 11, 2016, https://blogs.chapman.edu/press-room/2016/10/11/what-do-americans-fear-most-chapman-universitys-third-annual-survey-of-american-fears-released/ .

know I'm a liberal? Do I have a sign on my forehead that says: "I'm a liberal!" Then a sadness came over me. This meant that the people in this household only wanted to be with people who were like them. Even if I wanted to have a meaningful conversation with them to achieve mutual understanding, the chance of that happening was minimal. Perhaps the sign on the fence is a sign of our times. It signaled to me that the fear-exploiters had successfully isolated people, fostering fear and phobia of the other to the point of ignoring history and factual truth, creating many fear-conquerors who strike back in ways that strip others of their constitutional rights, targeting scapegoats like the immigrants and forcing the poor and powerless to be fear-bearers.

While I was feeling self-righteous about what I just wrote, I realized I might be as guilty as the person who put up the "Liberal Free Zone" sign. Have I not also isolated or insulated myself from those who are politically different from me? Even though I don't have a sign that says, "Conservative Free Zone" in front of my house, or my church, I wonder if I do have an invisible sign that says just that. I, too, have a fear of the others that causes me to insulate myself and not hear and know the others' truth. How many conservative friends do I really know?

The people of the United States are so polarized that it is almost like we live in separate countries. All one needs to do is look at the map of the 2016 election results. We listen and are influenced by totally different sets of "truths," which are more like a litany of fears of the other. Some are imminent and most are not. Most people are so overwhelmed by the nonstop projections of fear that we stop trying to discern which are imminent and which are mostly a distraction.

In the 2017 Chapman University survey, researchers learned that "three out of five Americans report they are very afraid or afraid that Islamic extremists/jihadists are a threat to national security. After Islamic extremists/jihadists, white supremacists are the only group that a majority of Americans view as a threat to national security (51 percent). On further investigation, researchers discover that Republicans are more likely to view Islamic extremists as a threat (83 percent) while Democrats are more concerned with white supremacists (74 percent). The answers to questions about which extremists are viewed as national security threats confirm this isolation and polarization among the different political groups in the U.S.

A divided and isolated population becomes more vulnerable to the manipulations of the fear-exploiters and marketers who feed different facts and untruths to different groups so that people within these groups continue to be fearful or even develop a phobia for the other. Meanwhile we, the fear-bearers, might even be willing to let our civil liberties be taken away without a fight. The 2017 Chapman University survey also showed that "One-third agree or strongly agree with the statement, 'In order to curb terrorism in this country, it will be necessary to give up some civil liberties.' Even more, 35 percent, disagree or strongly disagree with the statement, 'We should preserve our freedoms even if it increases the risk of terrorism.' As has been seen before, elevated fears over national security can lead to lower support for national values."[19]

Forming diverse community across the divides, building relationship among people who are different or even fearful of each other, and engaging them in courageous conversation are the most important things that we can do to foster wellness in this truth-distorting, divisive, fear-upon-fear age. It's also the Christian thing to do. But how do we do this when we are so divided? We are treating each other like people who were considered "unclean" in the Bible; yet Jesus spent a fair amount of time with those considered "unclean" during his ministry on earth. So as followers of Jesus, how do we make it happen in this age?

One Bridge at a Time

Before the 2016 election, a friend of mine had noticed a campaign sign in his next-door neighbor's front yard supporting the other candidate. He did not know this neighbor well except for the safe "good mornings" and "nice weather" talks. He speculated that she was a nice person. But like most of us, he had avoided any kind of political conversation with her during this time. After the election, he realized that he did not know anyone who had voted differently than himself, and decided to do something about this, beginning with getting to know his neighbor. The next morning, after saying "good morning," he proposed to his neighbor that they should have tea or coffee, and that he wanted to understand her perspective. To his surprise, she said yes.

[19]Sheri Ledbetter, "What do Americans Fear Most? Chapman University Releases 4th Annual Survey of American Fears," Chapman University, October 11, 2017, https://blogs.chapman.edu/press-room/2017/10/11/what-do-americans-fear-most/ .

That's how we begin—building one bridge with one person at a time. I challenge all my readers to find the courage to invite at least one person with different political views for a one-on-one, respectful conversation this week. Here are some helpful steps:

1. **Do your homework:** Take some time to reflect on why you voted the way you did (or if you didn't vote, why?) and consider the impact of the last election on you personally, on your family, your work, your friends, your community, etc. Pay attention to your "hot buttons." What would send you into a defensive, angry, and combative mode? Mentally prepare yourself on how to avoid going there, and how to get back to a more curious and open mindset for dialogue, if you are triggered. Formulate your reflections into "I" statements. This way, you are claiming your own experience when you share, while avoiding judgment of the other, which usually shuts down communication. Try completing these sentences:

    a. I voted for _____ because I _____.

    b. When I realized that _____ had been elected, I _____.

    c. With the elected person in office, my life is _____ , my family _____, my friends _____, my work _____, and my community _____.

2. **Write a gracious invitation.** Here is a sample:

    I know we have very different political viewpoints. However, I would like to invite you to _____ (coffee or lunch) to have a real conversation for half an hour about our experiences in this very divided time within our nation. I will listen to your experience and perspective. I will not argue or try to convince you of my position. I would invite you to do the same for me if you agree to share. I want to do this because I believe we both love this country, and as neighbors (or coworkers, classmates, family, friends), we can at least understand each other and maybe even find some common ground to work together for the good of our _____ (community, company, family, country, etc.).

3. **Set parameters and ground rules:** Before you start the conversation at the agreed upon time and place, take your responsibility for setting down some guidelines for the conversation. If it is appropriate, you can use the Respectful

Communication Guidelines[20] provided by the Kaleidoscope Institute and walk through the guidelines with your conversation partner. For a conversational way to set some helpful ground rules, try this:

- I would like us to have an honest, thoughtful conversation and not a debate about who is right or wrong, because I really want to understand your perspective and experience, and I hope you want to understand mine as well.
- Can we agree to share our own experiences and not try to defend anyone else or a whole party?
- Can we agree not to be dismissive of each other's experiences? Can we not judge, blame, and shame each other?
- Can we not interrupt each other and let each other finish our thoughts before responding?
- Can we agree to hang in there even when we don't quite understand each other's perspective yet, and try to ask clarifying questions of each other?

   (Note: if your conversation partner cannot agree to some kind of guidelines for communication, walk away.)

4. **Start with insightful questions:** Don't begin the conversation by asking right-wrong, good-bad questions. Start with information-seeking questions that assist both of you to share your interests, values, and beliefs. Try these:

   a. What is most important to you in your political beliefs?

   b. What are the hopes, concerns, and values that are at the heart of your beliefs?

   c. What life experiences have led you to believe the things you do?

      (Once you both are able to share your values and beliefs, you can go into more specific questions about the election.)

   d. How did your values and beliefs lead you to vote the way you did in the last election?

   e. What are the strengths and gifts of your candidate? What are his or her weaknesses?

---

[20]I first published the Respectful Communication Guidelines in Eric H. F. Law, *The Bush Was Blazing But Not Consumed* (St. Louis: Chalice Press, 1996), 87. You can also find the guidelines in Spanish, French, Chinese, and Korean in the Kaleidoscope Institute website: http://www.kscopeinstitute.org/respectful-communication-guidelines/ .

    f. *(If you're speaking after an election),* Now that [*elected person*] is in office, what are your hopes for the coming years?

    g. What are your concerns and fears for the coming years?

    h. In what ways can we stay friends and even support each other in the midst of our differences in the coming years?

5. **Feedback and stay curious:** When the conversation gets sidetracked, or when you feel stuck and want to strike back, or when you just don't get it, stop, take a deep breath and refocus by asking yourself: Am I really listening? Am I only listening to what I wanted to hear and looking for the other's faults? Try to put yourself back in that "curious" place again and remind yourself that the purpose of this conversation is for you to understand the other, not necessarily agree. Let your conversation partner know that you are trying to understand by giving feedback and ask clarifying questions. Try these:

    a. Let me make sure I understand what you mean. You are saying that this is important to you because _____. Is that right?

    b. (Example of clarifying questions) How did you come to believe that? Was there an experience that led you to believe that? Why is that important to you?

    I found the following helpful chart of don'ts and dos from a resource called "Reaching the Red/Blue Divide" presented by Essential Partners.[21]

Don't	Do
Tell them they are wrong	Ask them what value led them there
Ask how they could ever believe something	Ask when that belief first started for them
Interrupt people	Give a moment to make sure they are done
Say, "Yeah, but, what about..."	Say, "Huh, interesting, tell me more..."
Try to assume you know their motives	Ask about their goals and hopes
Blame them for your anger or frustration	Explain your frustration and take responsibility for it

---

[21]"A USA TODAY NETWORK Guide: Reaching across the red/blue divide," https://gallery.mailchimp.com/55d30ed01081c2d4d315e26de/files/Red_Blue_Divide_Guide.pdf?utm_source=General+Mailing+List&utm_campaign=83659bf5ac-EMAIL_CAMPAIGN_2016_11_10&utm_medium=email&utm_term=0_f75e5446ba-83659bf5ac-40621729)

6. **Thank your conversation partner:** When the conversation comes to a natural stopping place, share what you have learned from this conversation and invite your conversation partner to do the same. Then thank the other for being willing to enter into a truthful conversation with you. If appropriate, pray together and set another time to further the conversation.

I know this seems like a lot of work, but it is worth the time and energy if we really want to build bridges across our differences. If 1,000 of you build a little bridge with 1,000 people on the other side, the bridge will get a little wider and stronger. If the 2,000 people had a good experience and decided to reach out to another 2,000 people with a similar process, we will double the strength of our bridge, and so on. But it requires that every one of these conversations be constructive and regenerative, and that means we need to be courageous and disciplined in our invitation and facilitation of these dialogues.

In 2016 I began creating a resource called Building Bridges Now: Dialogue on Race and Other Important Issues of our Time.[22] It consists of carefully designed dialogue sessions that are intended to be a cohesive dialogue program inviting participants to commit to recurring sessions covering topics such as Race and Children, Race and Privilege, Black Lives Matter, Race and Immigration, Stop and Frisk, Stand Your Ground, etc. The sessions are designed for facilitators with limited training (at least two days provided by the Kaleidoscope Institute). Facilitators are required to use the "scripted" format to give instructions for each dialogue segment. (See sample dialogue in the Appendix.) That is, read the italic paragraphs as if they are the script of a play. We do this because we want to ensure that the instructions are given clearly without the facilitators having to learn it by heart or give them extemporaneously. Our goal is to have trained facilitators in lots of churches who can create gracious time and space for people with diverse backgrounds to come together to have a meaningful, constructive conversation.

Included in the Appendix is a full script of a Building Bridge Now dialogue session titled "Prep for the Holidays." This session invites participants to explore ways to engage friends and relatives in constructive conversations during holiday gatherings, especially when politics comes up. You can also access another session, titled "Disaster Preparedness," by going to ChalicePress.com/FearNot and

---

[22]Go to www.buildingbridgesnow.com for more information on this curriculum and facilitator training.

downloading the full process. This session brings people together to learn to be disaster-ready and to have conversations about how to be a supportive community in case of a disaster.

The Dialogue Song

If God loves me
And God loves you,
What happens when we disagree?
What are we gonna do?

What are we gonna do?

If I listen to you
And you listen to me,
In between your words and mine,
We may hear the Word of God divine.
If you walk with me
And I walk with you,
In between my way and yours,
We can find the sacred path
That leads to many gracious open doors

If God loves me
And God loves you,
What happens when we disagree?
What are we gonna do?
What are we gonna do?

If I see what you see
And you see what I see,
In between your view and mine,
We may see the view of God's design.
If you know my fears
And I know your fears
In between my fears and yours,
We can build a place that's safe
Where justice reigns with grace and not with wars.

If God loves me
And God loves you,
What happens when we disagree?
What are we gonna do?
What are we gonna do?

Disaster Preparedness

Back to Lake Arrowhead where I was standing in front of the house with the "Liberal Free Zone" sign when a question came to me: "If a super storm or a huge earthquake hit Lake Arrowhead and my house was destroyed, would the people in this house help me, even though I am not like them? Or if their house was destroyed, would they let me help them?" The answer is, of course, yes.

Natural disasters, destructive as they are, tend to unify communities and even nations. A storm like Hurricane Harvey didn't care whether one was a Republican or Democrat, rich or poor, citizen or immigrant, documented or undocumented, gay or straight or transgender. The storm just blew wind and poured rain on everyone. A natural disaster brings out the need for compassion and cooperation in order for people in any community to survive together.

Even the U.S. Immigration and Customs Enforcement and U. S. Customs and Border Protection understand this. Both departments issued a joint statement before Harvey made landfall the first time: "The Department's law enforcement components will be at the ready to help anyone in need of assistance. . . . Routine non-criminal immigration enforcement operations will not be conducted at evacuation sites, or assistance centers such as shelters or food banks." The full statement was translated into Spanish, Chinese, Korean and Vietnamese. They wanted to make sure that people who don't speak English got this message. Similar statements have been issued before other hurricanes since Harvey too.[23]

We often refer to natural disasters as acts of God. Perhaps this is what Paul means when he said in the letter to the Romans, "Leave room for the wrath of God" (Rom. 12:19). Perhaps God is angry at the way we, humankind, messed up the life-giving cycle that God had created for this earth. In a polarizing world or mindset, we are always looking for an enemy, someone to blame when something bad happens. If another country drops a bomb on our land, we can point our fingers at them, say they are the enemy, vow to retaliate, and drop a bomb on them. This is how wars start—with polarized, binary thinking.

An act of God, in the form of a natural disaster, throws a loop into that kind of thinking because we can't really point the finger

[23]"ICE says it will not conduct immigration enforcement operations in affected areas during Hurricane Dorian," *USA Today,* Aug. 20, 2019. https://www.usatoday.com/story/news/politics/2019/08/30/ice-immigration-enforcement-operations-during-dorian/2168682001/ .

at God and say God is the enemy. We cannot really retaliate against God either. What would we do, create a storm and get back at God? In Proverbs 9:10, we read "The fear of [God] is the beginning of wisdom." Even when the earth reacts with destructive storms, God is still trying to teach us a lesson. And the lesson is: we need each other. We need to work together despite our differences to create a healthy, mutually supportive community.

But the forces of division are strong. Sometimes I fear that even the wrath of God may not teach us this wisdom. The day before our country faced a potentially devastating disaster, which in the past had been an opportunity for leaders to unify our country, President Trump did two things that further polarized the people of our nation: (1) pardoning Sheriff Joe Arpaio of Maricopa County, Arizona, who was convicted of criminal contempt of court for racial profiling; and (2) directing the Pentagon to begin the process of banning transgender Americans from serving in the military. Whether or not Trump was conscious of what he was doing, he launched a preemptive strike on unity. It's as if he was saying to the people, "Before you come together to support each other to face this storm, I am going to make sure you are divided."

Unity of the people is what fear-exploiters fear the most. Throughout history, dictators have ruled by dividing people, destroying their ability to come together, out of fear projected onto each other. As long as the people were fighting each other, a dictator maintained his power in the midst of chaos. I hope the U.S. Constitution can guarantee that the presidency will never be a dictatorship. But we need to pay attention to the evil, divisive forces at work in our country, which look a lot like what a totalitarian government would do to its people. I think we can all agree, independent of our political affiliation, that the divisive forces are getting stronger, and we have become more isolated and divided. I think we can also agree that we have been coerced into fighting each other more and more since the beginning of 2017.

Earlier I asked the question: Who stands to gain from people not taking the fear of natural disaster seriously? Perhaps the ones who benefit from our inaction on this fear are the fear-exploiters who do not want people to form communities of mutual care, sharing, and cooperation. The good news in the midst of the bad news is this: despite any preemptive strikes on unity, people across the country and especially in Texas have stayed united in helping each other through the storm and in the recovery process.

So one way to counter these divisive forces is to gather people in community for disaster preparedness. I call this movement a preemptive strike on divisiveness.

We can start a movement by facilitating Community Disaster Preparedness events in every local community across the nation. In addition to sharing vital information on what to do in case of a disaster, invite people to connect with each other on a most basic human level. Invite them to consider what they would share in order to help the community survive together.

Each one of us can do a little preemptive strike on division by finding the courage to reach across whatever divides us. The person on the other side might be a family member, a neighbor, a person in church who sits on the other side, a coworker, a classmate. Again, start with the basics: what would we do with and for each other in case of a disaster? What common ground can we stand on in order to get through the disaster together? Through this conversation, we might find opportunities to share our love for this land, and share our experiences of what different divisive forces are doing to our personal lives and our communities. In the process of sharing our truths, we might find the common truth that we can speak together and from which to take action to return our country to its original calling: *people are endowed by their Creator with certain unalienable Rights, that among these are Life, Liberty and the pursuit of Happiness.*

This is not going to be easy. It requires us to take down our visible and invisible fear-based signs that say "conservative free zone" or "liberal free zone" and become vulnerable. It will feel like we might lose our lives if we open ourselves up to listen to another who has a different and even opposing view on life, community, and nations. Yet that's what is required of us in Jesus' call to love our neighbor as ourselves and to love our enemy. It requires us to take what Paul shared in the letter to the Romans as a roadmap:

> Rejoice in hope, be patient in suffering, persevere in prayer....extend hospitality to strangers. Bless those who persecute you; bless and do not curse them. Rejoice with those who rejoice, weep with those who weep. Live in harmony with one another; do not be haughty, but associate with the lowly; do not claim to be wiser than you are. Do not repay anyone evil for evil, but take thought for what is noble in the sight of all. If it is possible, so far as it depends on you, live peaceably with all. Beloved, never

avenge yourselves, but leave room for the wrath of God. (Romans 12:12–19)

Christians can be courageous people because we are not afraid of death. Jesus' story did not end on the cross. The finale is the Resurrection. We Christians can hold on to that hope of resurrection and therefore have the courage to walk the difficult, uneasy road. That's how you launch a preemptive strike on the principalities and powers that seek to divide us, separating us from each other and from God. "For I am convinced that neither death, nor life, nor angels, nor rulers, nor things present, nor things to come, nor powers, nor height, nor depth, nor anything else in all creation, will be able to separate us from the love of God in Christ Jesus our Lord" (Romans 8:38–39).

Let Go of Your Fears

Set your troubled hearts at rest
And let go of your fears
'Cause all of you are blessed
Your strengths, your faults and your tears
So let go of your fears

We've got ev'rything we need
So drop your shields and spears
Let mercy take the lead
Let truth and grace be our cheers
And let go of your fears

Don't let fear kill your curiosity
Don't let fear take away your bravery
Don't let fear make you build dividing walls
'Cause in God's house, there are many rooms,
Rooms for one and all
So let go of your fears

Hold on fast to what is true
That's how we persevere
We'll let our truth shine through
For dark time's not welcome here
Let go of your fears

We've got power from above

No more fear of fears
The power is called love, yes love
Share your love, God is here
Let go of your fears

Activities and Questions for Discussion:

1. Try Thich Nhat Hanh's "five remembrances" breathing exercise (pp. 101–102) for at least five minutes. Take time to breathe deeply into each one of the truth statements. What insights did you receive by doing this exercise?

2. Try posting or reposting a factual or experienced truth with the hashtag #3MillionTruth to counter an untruth, misinformation, or lies being spread on social media. Encourage your followers and friends to do the same. Check the next day or week to see if you have started a wave of truth.

3. Review the top ten fears of 2015, 2016, 2017, and 2018. What do you notice? What do you wonder about? Share your reflections.

4. Complete the charts for analyzing the 2016 and 2017 top ten fears. What do you notice? What do you wonder about? Share your reflections.

5. Complete the chart rating the level of imminence of the 2018 top ten fears.
   a. Which ones have high ratings (a combined score between 6 and 10)? What will you do about these fears?
   b. Which ones have low ratings (a combined score between 2 and 5)? What will you do about these fears?
   c. Name other fears that you have and do the rating on them. What do you notice?

6. How have you experienced being isolated and insulated from people and groups who are politically different from you? What can you do to create an opportunity for a courageous and gracious conversation with people on the other side?

7. Using the process described in the "One Bridge at a Time" section of the chapter, write a gracious invitation to invite a person who voted differently from you during a recent election to enter into dialogue with you. Share your experience and reflection.

8. Record the first ten minutes of prime time news from two major cable news networks such as Fox News, CNN, or MSNBC.

Gather friends with different political affiliations and watch the news segments together. What are the differences between the two ten-minute segments in terms of emphases and order of the stories? Was there a difference between the two in terms of what fears were employed to get your attention? If they reported on the same story, what were the differences between the two reports? Why were there differences? If possible, do a fact check on the story together.

9. Contact the Kaleidoscope Institute to coordinate a Building Bridges Now facilitator training in your area. Invite churches in your area to participate by sending leaders to be trained. Working with a co-facilitator, facilitate a dialogue session for a group of diverse friends using the Appendix, especially before a major holiday where there will be gatherings of friends and family. Please read all the instructions carefully. You also need to make sure you have the technology and equipment to show the videos for the dialogue sessions.

10. Coordinate with other churches and community organizations to create a disaster preparedness event for the people in your neighborhood using the dialogue session material available as a free download at ChalicePress.com/FearNot.

Appendix

Building Bridges Now

In 2016 I began creating a resource called Building Bridges Now: Dialogue on Race and Other Important Issues of our Time. It consists of carefully designed dialogue sessions that are intended to be a cohesive program inviting participants to commit to recurring sessions covering topics such as Race and Children, Race and Privilege, Black Lives Matter, Race and Immigration, Stop and Frisk, Stand Your Ground, etc. The sessions are designed for facilitators with limited training (at least two days provided by the Kaleidoscope Institute). Facilitators are required to use the "scripted" format to give instructions for each dialogue segment. That is, read the italic paragraphs as if they are the script of a play. We do this because we want to ensure that the instructions are given clearly without the facilitators having to learn it by heart or give them extemporaneously.

Our goal is to have trained facilitators in lots of churches who can create gracious time and space for people with diverse backgrounds to come together to have a meaningful, constructive conversation.

This Appendix includes the full "Prep for the Holidays" dialogue session. To access another full session, titled "Disaster Preparedness," go to ChalicePress.com/FearNot to download. Also, go to BuildingBridgesNow.com for more information on the full curriculum and facilitator training.

Prep for the Holidays[1]

Objective: To invite participants into a gracious time and space to have a constructive dialogue on preparing ourselves and others for gracious and courageous conversations during holiday gatherings.

Type of Group: Adults from diverse backgrounds (race, ethnicity, age, gender, economic status, political affiliations, etc.)

Size of Group: six to twelve

Setting: A bright, large room with empty wall space for posting chart paper. Chairs for participants should be arranged in circle, with a clear view of the chart paper and video screen.

Material: Session handouts, sturdy writing surface (such as a cardboard or clipboard for each person), pens/pencils. Equipment for video presentation. Chart paper and dark markers (water-washable are best).

Time Required: two to three hours depending on the size of the group

Preparation:
Before participants arrive,

    a.   Post pieces of chart paper on the wall (Conocimiento[2] Chart) with the following categories across the top:

        Name
        My favorite holiday gathering is . . . because . . .
        When difficult topics came up in holiday gatherings, I . . .
        In order for me to have gracious and courageous conversation,
        I . . .

    b.   Write the reflection questions for the video on chart paper:

---

[1]"Prep for the Holidays" is from Building Bridges Now, a carefully designed dialogue online curriculum provided by the Kaleidoscope Institute. See BuildingBridgesNow.com for information.

[2]*Conocimiento* is the Spanish word for knowledge. This was the name of a process my colleagues learned when they were working in Central America in the 1970s. They passed this tool on to me when they trained me to be a dialogue facilitator. This is a great process to help participants focus on the dialogue topic as they arrive.

For second video:

- *What stood out for you as you watched this video?*
- *What do you appreciate most from this video?*
- *What does it take for you to listen beyond what feels like an attack?*
- *What does it take for you to stay curious?*

Set Up the Video: "Conflict is a Place of Possibility" by Dana Caspersen—Contact the Kaleidoscope Institute office at kscope@kscopeinstitute.org to get the password to the link to this video on our website. You can also download this video from YouTube at: https://www.youtube.com/watch?v=WfQeH3092Sc

Overview of Dialogue Process

- Welcome, opening reflection, and setting parameters for dialogue
- Introduce (or review) Respectful Communication Guidelines
- Focusing text: Excerpt from *The Book of Forgiving* by Desmond Tutu and Mpho Tutu
- Introduction using *Conocimiento* chart and Mutual Invitation
- First Dialogue Process: Preparation for dialogue: Know Your Story
- Second Dialogue Process: "Conflict is a Place of Possibility" by Dana Caspersen
- Practice clarifying questions
- A word about hosting a holiday gathering
- Commitment for future participation
- Closing and sending

How to Proceed:

1. As participants arrive, invite each one to take a marker and complete the Conocimiento charts.
2. Welcome and Opening Reflection:

   A facilitator invites participants to sit in the circle of chairs and read the following:

   Welcome to Building Bridges Now. This program is sponsored by _____ and the Kaleidoscope Institute to provide a gracious space to have constructive conversations in our community on race relations and other important issues of our time. The purpose of dialogue is to bring together people with diverse backgrounds, viewpoints, and experiences to have meaningful conversation on a common subject.

We invite you to enter into a time of dialogue, remembering that:
- *Dialogue does not force anyone to change. It is not a debate in which we try to convince others that we are right. It is about mutual understanding.*
- *Dialogue is NOT about finger pointing, demonizing or punishing individuals or groups. True dialogue invites each one of us to commit to sharing his or her truth while being willing to listen deeply to another's truth.*
- *Dialogue does not avoid our history and present differences, pretending that everything is okay. Dialogue acknowledges our history and our present differences. By sharing our different experiences, we can achieve greater understanding of the issue and move toward potential reconciliation, fostering constructive change in our community.*

3. Respectful Communication Guidelines[3]

Hand out copies of the Respectful Communication Guidelines. A facilitator gives the following explanation: (Note: an abbreviated version can be used if there are no new members joining the group since the last gathering.)

We, people from different cultural backgrounds, bring with us different assumptions of communication styles. Sometimes these different assumptions may cause communication breakdown. Therefore, before we begin our dialogue, I invite you to consider a set of Respectful Communication Guidelines. They are written in the acronym from the word "RESPECT."

Two or more facilitators may take turns reading the following explanation of the Respectful Communication Guidelines.

R = *take RESPONSIBILITY for what you say and feel without blaming others*
Avoid judgmental language, which can cause defensiveness and cut off communication. Instead, use "I" statements. Begin what you want to say with "I," claiming what is

---

[3]I first published the Respectful Communication Guidelines in Eric H. F. Law, *The Bush Was Blazing but Not Consumed* (St. Louis: Chalice Press, 1996), 87. You can also find the guidelines in Spanish, French, Chinese and Korean in the Kaleidoscope Institute website: http://www.kscopeinstitute.org/free-resources.

yours. For example, I feel, I know, I believe, I think, I notice, I wonder, etc.

E = use EMPATHETIC listening
Put yourself in the other person's shoes and attempt to see and experience the issue from the speaker's perspective. This is a commitment that we make to try as hard as we can to understand each other, knowing our limits. Therefore, it is okay to ask clarifying questions. It is also okay to give feedback to check if you have understood what the speaker was saying.

S = be SENSITIVE to differences in communication styles
When someone behaves differently from you, don't simply interpret that behavior using your own assumptions about what is good communication. Remind yourself that this person might be communicating in a very different way and there might be opportunities to learn more about how the other communicates.

P = PONDER what you hear and feel before you speak
Think before you speak.

E = EXAMINE your own assumptions and perceptions
As you ponder, ask yourself what caused you to feel, think, or react in a certain way. Where might these ideas come from for you? If you are able to notice your own assumptions, you are more able to take responsibility for your own thinking and feeling.

C = keep CONFIDENTIALITY
In order to uphold the well-being of each person in this group, I invite you to keep the personal information shared here in confidence.
This way, we can feel safer in talking about real issues that concern our lives and our communities without the fear that they might be shared outside without the full benefit of the trust developed in this group.

T = TRUST ambiguity because we are NOT here to debate who is right or wrong.
In order to address these issues constructively, we must be willing and able to listen to each other's different experiences and points of view even though at times, the

ambiguity might be uncomfortable for some of us. By listening empathically without judgment and debate, we, as a community, may gain a fuller description of the issues we are trying address. In this way, instead of being divided, we can move forward, working together to find constructive ways to address them.

After the reading of the explanations, a facilitator asks participants if there are questions and then poses the following question:

Do we have an agreement to uphold these guidelines for the rest of our time together? I need a sign or gesture from all of you to indicate that you agree.

If nobody disagrees, the facilitator can continue with the dialogue process. If there are questions, discuss it until there is an agreement, and then continue with the dialogue process.

Problems to Anticipate in this section:
Be prepared to give concrete behavioral examples if there are questions about the meaning of the guidelines.

In this dialogue session, we will have opportunities to prepare ourselves and others for gracious and courageous conversations during holiday gatherings. To help us focus our time together, I would like to read an excerpt from The Book of Forgiving *by Desmond Tutu and Mpho Tutu. Archbishop Desmond Tutu is a South African Anglican cleric and theologian known for his work as an anti-apartheid and human rights activist. Mpho Tutu is an Episcopal Priest and founding Director of the Desmond & Leah Tutu Legacy Foundation:*

> *Can you hold that space open for me?*
> *Can you keep your questions and suggestions*
> *And judgments at bay?*
> *Can you wait with me for the truths that stay*
> *Hidden behind my sadness, my fear, my forgetting, and my pain?*
> *Can you just hold open a space for me to tell my story?*[4]

4Desmond Tutu and Mpho Tutu, *The Book of Forgiving* (HarperOne, 2015), 89.

4. Introduction Process:

A facilitator gives the following instructions to introduce the process. (Note: if there are no new members joining the group, simply remind participants that we will be using Mutual Invitation again for the next process and skip the detailed instructions. If the group is bigger than twelve, you will need to divide the group into smaller groups of no more than twelve with a facilitator for each group giving the following instructions.)

In order to help us get to know each other better, I invite you to introduce yourselves using the categories on the wall chart, which you filled out when you arrived.

In order to ensure that everyone who wants to share HAS the opportunity to speak, we will use a process called Mutual Invitation[5]:

The leader or a designated person shares first. After that person has spoken, he or she then invites another to share. Try not to invite the person next to you so that we won't move into the habit of going around in a circle. After the next person has spoken, that person is given the privilege to invite another to share.

If you are not ready to share, say "I pass for now," and we will invite you to share later on. If you don't want to say anything at all, simply say "pass" and proceed to invite another to share. We will do this until everyone has been invited.

We invite you to listen and not to respond to someone's sharing immediately. There will be time to respond and to ask clarifying questions after everyone has shared.

Any questions?

A facilitator may decide to demonstrate the Mutual Invitation process by inviting the group to share "What is your favorite ice cream?"

We have set aside about ____ minutes for this process. That means each person will have ____ minutes to share. I will ask you to respect other people's time as you share. Are there any questions?

[5] I first introduced Mutual Invitation in Eric H. F. Law, *The Wolf Shall Dwell with the Lamb* (St. Louis: Chalice Press, 1993), 79–88. It is now one of the principal gracious skills in all our dialogue processes. You can find this process described in Spanish, French, and Chinese at the Kaleidoscope Institute website, http://www.kscopeinstitute.org/free-resources.

Facilitator then begins the process by introducing him/herself.

When everyone has introduced themselves, the facilitator debriefs the group by asking participants to complete the sentences:

> *I noticed. . .*
> *I wonder . . .*

Problems to anticipate in this section: People sometimes forget to invite others after they finish speaking. Do not invite for them. Simply remind them they have the privilege to invite the next person.

Break

5. Preparation for Dialogue: Know Your Story

Facilitators invite participants to return to their seats and pass out the reflection sheet: Preparation for Dialogue: Know Your Story.

> *In order to have gracious and courageous dialogue with others, especially those with whom we disagree, we need to know our own story—our feeling, values, beliefs and assumptions. If we know ourselves, we will be secure enough to listen to the differing others without the fear of losing ourselves. Using the worksheet Preparation for Dialogue: Know Your Story, I invite you to name up to four issues (across the first row of the chart) in the last year that might cause conflicts in conversation during holiday gatherings. For example, the U.S. Presidential election, sexual harassment, health care, tax reform, climate change, Russian meddling, etc.*
>
> *For each issue, fill in the column by answering the questions using "I" statements, which will help you claim your own experience when you share while avoiding making judgment on the other, which can shut down communication.*

Give time for participants to reflect and/or write on the worksheet/handout.

> *We've set aside ___ minutes to share our reflections from this worksheet. We'll use Mutual Invitation for this. Please share only what you are comfortable sharing with the group. Each person will have about ___ minutes to share.*

Break (Facilitators set up the video "Conflict Is a Place of Possibility," a TedX talk available on YouTube. Have the video ready to be played.)

6. Dialogue Using the Video: "Conflict is a Place of Possibility" by Dana Caspersen

    Facilitators invite participants to return to their seats to view the video. Hand out reflection sheet for the video.

    Before the next round of sharing, I would like to invite us to read the following excerpt from The Book of Forgiving *by Desmond Tutu and Mpho Tutu:*

    > *Can you hold that space open for me?*
    > *Can you keep your questions and suggestions*
    > *And judgments at bay?*
    > *Can you wait with me for the truths that stay*
    > *Hidden behind my sadness, my fear, my forgetting, and my pain?*
    > *Can you just hold open a space for me to tell my story?*

    Facilitators play the video.

    I now invite you to ponder these questions:

    - *What stood out for you as you watched this video?*
    - *What do you appreciate most from this video?*
    - *What does it take for you to listen beyond what feels like an attack?*
    - *What does it take for you to stay curious?*

    Give participants time to ponder the questions.

    Using Mutual Invitation, let's briefly share our responses to the questions.

    Facilitators distribute the handouts: Developing Your Currency of Relationship and Stay Curious: Ask Clarifying Questions

    The handout "Developing Your Currency of Relationship" is a page from the book Drawing on Holy Currencies *by Eric Law and Dave Law. One of the keys to staying curious and not being judgmental is to know how to ask clarifying questions. (Referring to the handout.) We begin with creating opportunities for formal and/or informal conversations. So in your future holiday gathering, you can create such opportunities, especially if you are the host. Later on in this session, we will share with you some ideas on how to frame your gatherings for constructive conversation.*

Start or strengthen a relationship by paying attention to the person. Be curious and discover the person's self-interest by listening without judgment. Help the person clarify his/her self-interest by asking clarifying questions.

A clarifying question is based on three simple principles:
— It comes from genuine curiosity.
— It seeks information and understanding.
— It reserves judgment.
Finally, let the person know you have been listening by giving feedback.

Let's practice clarifying questions using the handout: Stay Curious - Ask Clarifying Questions. I invite you to write up to two statements that you have heard that puzzled or confused or caused you to have strong reactions. These can be about any of the issues that you had named earlier.

Give participate time to write.
Below each of the statements, write down some potential clarifying questions. Remember that these questions seek information and understanding and are nonjudgmental. On the second half of the worksheet, we have included some helpful don'ts and dos.

Give participate time to write.
Using Mutual Invitation, I invite you to share at least one of your statements and your suggested clarifying questions. The rest of the group can offer suggestions as well.

7.   A Word about Being a Host of a Holiday Gathering

As a host, you can gather your guests and frame the gathering with something like the Respectful Communication Guidelines. For example, you can share or post the Don'ts and Dos of conversations or you can get handout bookmarks with the Respectful Communication Guidelines. Contact the Kaleidoscope Institute if you want some of the RESPECT bookmarks for your event.

*In your welcome "address" to your guests, you can say,
"Welcome to our home. In this house, we invite you to you get
to know each other despite differences. Living in an increasingly
divided and polarized world, we often avoid sharing who we
are and what we believe during family gatherings out of a fear
that we might cause conflicts and trouble. But if we don't share
these things about ourselves, we will be further alienated from
each other. Having honest conversation is not about winning an
argument; it is about achieving understanding without having
to agree with each other. So when difficult topics come up, and
they will, I invite you to practice these guidelines I learned from
the Building Bridges Now dialogue process . . ." Then you can
go over the guidelines briefly and the invite your guests to agree
to them.*

*This will feel strange and unnatural, but remember, you are
the host and you set the ground rules in your home.*

8. Reflection on the Experience

   Invite participants to recall what they learned from the
   last several hours and to consider the question:

   *What are you called to do in the next week or month
   especially during holiday gatherings?*

   Invite participants to share using Mutual Invitation.

9. Commitment to Future Participation

   Facilitators invite participants to take up different tasks
   for the next dialogue meeting:
   - host(s) at the meeting location
   - person(s) responsible for refreshments
   - If a meal is involved, assign responsibility for different
     parts of the meal
     for example, meat, vegetable, fruit, drink, dessert, . . .
     etc.
   - person(s) responsible for communication
   - transportation coordinator(s) if needed

10. Closing:

   Facilitators invite participants to take part in reading aloud
   the excerpt from *The Book of Forgiving by Desmond Tutu and*

Mpho Tutu:

Can you hold that space open for me?
Can you keep your questions and suggestions
And judgments at bay?
Can you wait with me for the truths that stay
Hidden behind my sadness, my fear, my forgetting, and my
    pain?
Can you just hold open a space for me to tell my story?

A facilitator invites participants to complete the sentences:

- *I am thankful today for . . .*
- *My hopes are . . .*

A facilitator invites participants to share their sentences using Mutual Invitation.

11. Sending Forth:

    A facilitator reads the following to send participants out into the world:

    Nourished by understanding
    Warmed by friends
    Fed by loved ones
    Matured by wisdom
    Tempered by tears
    Made holy by caring and sharing
    Go forth in peace![6]

    Adapted from Leonard Nimoy

12. Donation Request:

    If you appreciated this dialogue process, please make a donation to the Kaleidoscope Institute so that they can continue to develop more dialogue sessions and offer the Building Bridges Now resources to more people, including those who have limited financial resources.

---

[6]The first five lines are from a poem by **Leonard Nimoy. Leonard Nimoy Poetry, Photography, Quotations and Tweets,** http://www.thehypertexts.com/ Leonard%20Nimoy%20Poet%20Poetry%20Photographer%20Photography%20 Picture%20Literary%20Bio.htm

Respectful Communication Guidelines

R = Take RESPONSIBILITY for what you say and feel without blaming others

E = EMPATHETIC listening

S = Be SENSITIVE to differences in communication styles

P = PONDER what you hear and feel before you speak

E = EXAMINE your own assumptions and perceptions

C = Keep CONFIDENTIALITY (Share Constructively to uphold the well-being of COMMUNITY)

T = TOLERATE ambiguity because we are not here to debate who is right or wrong

(from *The Bush Was Blazing but Not Consumed* by Eric H. F. Law)

I agree to uphold these guidelines for the time we have together.

_____   _____
Signature   Date

Can you hold that space open for me?
Can you keep your questions and suggestions
And judgments at bay?
Can you wait with me for the truths that stay
Hidden behind my sadness, my fear, my forgetting, and my pain?
Can you just hold open a space for me to tell my story?

— *from* The Book of Forgiving *by Desmond Tutu*
    and Mpho Tutu

Reflection questions for the video:
"Conflict is a Place of Possibility"

- What stood out for you as you watched this video?

- What do you appreciate most from this video?

- What does it take for you to listen beyond what feels like an attack?

- What does it take for you to stay curious?

Preparation for Dialogue: Know Your Story

In order to be have gracious and courageous dialogue with others, especially those with whom we disagree, we need to know our own stories: our feelings, values, beliefs and assumptions. If we know ourselves, we will be secure enough to listen to the differing others without the fear of losing ourselves.

1. Name up to four issues (across the first row of the chart below) in the last year that might cause conflict in conversation during holiday gatherings. For example, the U.S. Presidential election, sexual harassment, health care, tax reform, climate change, Russian meddling, etc.
2. For each issue, fill in the column by answering the questions using an "I" statement.

ISSUES				
What was my initial reaction at the time this issue became prominent?	I . . .			
What were my assumptions/experiences that caused me to react the way I did? Where/when/from whom did I acquire these assumptions/experiences?	I . . .			
What was the most important thing about this issue for me?	I . . .			
Which of my values and beliefs were challenged or affirmed by this issue?	I . . .			

Stay Curious: Ask Clarifying Questions

Statements you have heard that puzzled and/or confused you:		
Write potential clarifying questions that seek information and are nonjudgmental:		

Helpful hints: (If you are hosting a gathering, you can share these don'ts and dos in a fun way with your guests as part of your welcome.)

Don't	Do
Tell them they are wrong	Ask them what value led them there
Ask how they could ever believe something	Ask when that belief first started for them
Interrupt people	Give a moment to make sure they are done
Say, "Yeah, but, what about..."	"Huh, interesting, tell me more..."
Try to assume you know their motives	Ask about their goals and hopes
Blame them for your anger or frustration	Explain your frustration and take responsibility for it

DEVELOPING YOUR CURRENCY OF RELATIONSHIP

CREATE OPPORTUNITIES FOR FORMAL AND/OR INFORMAL CONVERSATIONS.

START OR
STRENGTHEN
A RELATIONSHIP BY
PAYING ATTENTION
TO THE PERSON

HELP THE PERSON
CLARIFY HIS / HER
SELF - INTEREST BY
**ASKING CLARIFYING
QUESTIONS**

BE CURIOUS
AND DISCOVER THE
PERSON'S SELF-INTEREST
BY LISTENING WITHOUT
JUDGMENT.

WHAT'S A
CLARIFYING
QUESTION?

LET THE PERSON
KNOW YOU HAVE BEEN
LISTENING BY GIVING
FEEDBACK.

IT COMES
FROM GENUINE
CURIOSITY.

IT SEEKS
INFORMATION
AND
UNDERSTANDING.

IT
RESERVES
JUDGMENT.

TRY THIS PROCESS WITH SOMEONE YOU KNOW FOR 10 MINUTES. REPORT YOUR
EXPERIENCE HERE: